Wham! George & Me

ANDREW RIDGELEY

MICHAEL JOSEPH
an imprint of
PENGUIN BOOKS

MICHAEL JOSEPH

UK | USA | Canada | Ireland | Australia
India | New Zealand | South Africa

Michael Joseph is part of the Penguin Random House group of companies
whose addresses can be found at global.penguinrandomhouse.com.

First published by Michael Joseph, 2019
001

Copyright © Andrew Ridgeley, 2019

The moral right of the author has been asserted

Set in 13.5/16.2pt Garamond MT Std
Typeset by Jouve (UK), Milton Keynes
Printed and bound in Great Britain by Clays Ltd, Elcograf S.p.A.

A CIP catalogue record for this book is available from the British Library

HARDBACK ISBN: 978–0–241–38580–7
OM PAPERBACK ISBN: 978–0–241–38581–4

www.greenpenguin.co.uk

Penguin Random House is committed to a
sustainable future for our business, our readers
and our planet. This book is made from Forest
Stewardship Council® certified paper.

This memoir is dedicated to the memory of my dearest friend, with whom I did the only thing I ever really wanted to do and was the only person I ever imagined doing it with.

Introduction

The Long Goodbye

Saturday, 28 June 1986

I waited for George.

I always waited for George. This time, I was standing backstage at Wembley Stadium, patiently listening for my cue to make my entrance and waiting – *waiting, waiting, waiting.* The sun had melted below the arena's grand old twin towers and tens of thousands of people seemed to shimmer in the faraway corners of its bowl-shaped terraces. Others were pooled into a swaying, brightly coloured tide on the football pitch below. Teenage girls waved flags and home-made banners; camera flashbulbs popped as kids, couples and groups of families and friends screamed excitedly: seventy-two thousand fans drawn together at The Final, a farewell concert for Wham!, the youthful, hopeful, effervescent pop band that George and I had always intended to burn brightly, but briefly.

Four years on from the release of our first record in 1982, Wham! was still a big deal across radio, press and TV. Posters of me and George, pulled from the pages of *Smash Hits* and *Just Seventeen* magazine, had become the wallpaper for millions of teenage bedrooms, while showbiz columnists frothed over every snippet of Wham! news and gossip. But at the peak of our success, and after two studio albums and a portfolio of number 1 singles across the world, we were about to bid farewell to the very people drawn to those songs, those shows and those stories.

And all of them were waiting, waiting, waiting for the final show to begin.

I knew the routine backwards. George was onstage, walking towards the crowd, arms outstretched, striding along a catwalk that extended into Wembley's front rows. *This was his moment.* Dressed all in black, a blend of leather and denim, his swept-back hair offset by designer stubble, every gesture, every signal, became a call-and-response connection with the audience. George played to the crowd; they swooned. Flanked by two dancers, he moved and spun to the instrumental backdrop of 'Everything She Wants', the pulsing soundtrack to a showy, theatrical introduction. George loved performing this wry observation of married life, even though we had been young, single and unchained from responsibility at the time of its writing. He waved to fans in the farthest corners of Wembley's raucous

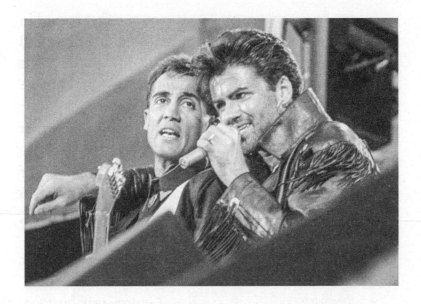

party. He turned his back on the audience, pointing seductively across the stage, the microphone yet to touch his lips. George hadn't said a word, let alone sung a note, but still everybody was hanging on his next move, a sensation I knew only too well.

Because I had spent so long waiting for George.

I'd waited for George as he endlessly readied himself for shows, teasing his hair with straighteners, sometimes for hours upon end while I recoiled at the acrid whiff of singed curls and hairspray in a ritual that appeared unnecessarily torturous. As our fame grew, George's appearance became a very serious matter. Prior to filming the video to 'Careless Whisper' in 1984, he even complained that his curly hair, an

uncontrollable mass of wiry frizz in the humidity, made him look 'like Shirley Bassey'. George's sister, Mel – a stylist – was then flown halfway around the world, from London to Miami, where the filming was taking place, to sculpt George's hair just the way he liked it. The bill for her flight and handiwork was reported to have been more than £10,000.

But I'd also waited for George as he worked through his frequent moments of musical inspiration. In the studio – a place where he toiled with an exacting attention to detail – or at home, when he would suddenly disappear for hours on end after being struck by some melodic cue or vocal hook. Often it proved to be yet another spark of genius, the most memorable snapshot of this process having taken place in February 1984 as we relaxed one Sunday afternoon in his parents' living room. *The Big Match* was on the telly but George's mind was very much on something other than football.

'I've got to go,' he said, jumping off the sofa and vanishing upstairs for over an hour.

When George returned, he was grinning proudly.

'Bloody hell, Andy,' he said, 'come upstairs, you've got to hear this . . .' He was excited, aware that he had composed something special, having worked out the basic arrangement and melody of a song he was loosely calling 'Last Christmas' on a four-track tape recorder – a demo he would eventually craft into the heart-bruised ballad that later became the biggest Christmas single not to make it to number 1. *God, that statistic annoyed him.* Despite its enduring success, the failure of 'Last Christmas' to topple the charity single by Band Aid that year – a musical union comprising, among others, Bob Geldof, U2, Duran Duran, Sting, Paul Weller and George himself – would irk him terribly, although he didn't begrudge the charity their success. Throughout his life, hit singles were regarded as the only affirmation of George's songwriting prowess and not being regarded as the best by his audience, or peers, was one of his greatest sources of irritation. But as we sat in his bedroom that day, the same place where we'd once analysed the Top 40 chart rundown after school as teenagers, I listened to a basic track that had been recorded on his synthesiser, its instantly memorable chorus hummed over the top, and beamed. George had captured the very heartbeat of Christmas, framing its lyrics within the pain of a broken romance.

And I'd waited for George as he transformed himself from the funny but occasionally introspective teenager Georgios Panayiotou firstly into Yog – the nickname I'd given to him soon after we'd met as classmates at Bushey Meads Comprehensive – and then into George Michael, the singer-songwriter and dearest friend of my formative years and beyond. As we embarked on an intense and unpredictable journey into the limelight, our bond strengthened further. George evolved into one of the defining voices of his generation. But while he was crafting some of the eighties' biggest singles, there was the sense that he was still defining himself. His sexuality remained a secret outside of Wham!'s inner circle and a gulf opened up between the very private life he was leading as a young gay man and his position as a teen pin-up and tabloid focus. He would later go on record as saying that the gravitational pull between private man and public personality created moments that threatened his sanity. Through all of this, I was a stable presence for George. He was my best friend and had been for years, but his personal destiny lay beyond the two of us. With Wham!'s last show at Wembley, the waiting for George was set to be over.

Likewise, with my life's ambitions achieved, it was over for me too.

I stepped down towards the catwalk, our backing singers Helen 'Pepsi' DeMacque and Shirlie Holliman alongside me. The screaming was deafening, the roar of Wembley becoming louder, much louder. As I walked towards the popping lights and surging crowd, I heard scattered voices from the front rows: shouts of 'Andrew!', or 'We love you, Wham!' But beyond that there was only white noise. I paused at the edge of the stage as the hysteria ricocheted around me. Wherever we went in the world, the reaction to our arrival onstage always struck me as extraordinary and I rarely took the fandom surrounding our music for granted, or too seriously. The screaming girls, the autograph-hunters and the paparazzi: all of it was hyper-real and strange. As a result, everything we did was played for laughs. George and I knew it was a game and we were always determined to play our part in giving our audiences the energy they loved – it was very much Wham!'s brand.

But in the weeks building up to it, The Final had been described as something of a near-religious event.

Fans were referred to as acolytes; Wham! as icons. In the early years, our look onstage was playful, cheeky, and our shows had made headlines for our too-short shorts and cropped T-shirts, while promo videos for songs such as 'Club Tropicana' were packed with tongue-in-cheek nods to the joys of youthful hedonism. However, at Wembley we'd decided to create a more dramatic mood to match the fervour, eschewing our usually vibrant stage image for a more severe tone. George wore skinny black jeans and leather boots. A belt glittered with rhinestones and his jacket, its collar up, had been trimmed with tassels. My all-black look was equally striking: with the help of Pepsi and Shirlie, I shrugged off my trench coat to reveal a high-cut, fringed, matador-style jacket, complete with boot-lace tie and sparkling belt. I struggled not to laugh as I slowly teased away my gloves, finger by finger, drop-ping them to the stage. Shirlie handed me my guitar and I pulled it over my shoulder. Showtime.

Both of us had appeared at Wembley before, so our surroundings were at least familiar. A year previously, I did backing vocals when George had sung at Live Aid, a charity gig that raised millions of pounds to help ease the famine in Ethiopia, just like Band Aid's Christmas single had done in 1984. That day had had an almost festival-like atmosphere. The Final also had a special, one-off feel to it, as tens of thousands of people flocked to London from all over the world, marking the end of a very colourful chapter in British music history.

The time for Wham! to say goodbye had arrived.

We played through the hits one last time. 'Club Tropi-cana', 'Bad Boys' and 'Edge of Heaven'; 'Wham Rap', 'Careless Whisper' and 'Freedom'. Stretching into the distance, the Wembley crowd looked as if they were ebbing and flowing, a huge pool of people singing and dancing together. In the build-up to our perfor-mance it was decided that we would sprinkle several surprises throughout the party, one of which was a cameo from Elton John, who joined us for a reworked version of his hit single 'Candle In The Wind'. The song had always emotionally resonated with the pair of us, having been a stand-out track on Elton's album *Goodbye Yellow Brick Road*, one of the records upon which our friendship was built. George was able to carry its melody beautifully, almost effortlessly, and while he considered himself a songwriter first and foremost, I always thought his greatest and most eloquent form of expression was his voice. From an early age it became his defining instrument and, as far as I was concerned, only Freddie Mercury stacked up against George as a vocalist at that time.

This wasn't the first time that George and Elton had performed together, either. At Live Aid, George had also sung 'Don't Let The Sun Go Down On Me' with Elton, and his band provided the backing track to George's towering vocal. But the relationship between George and Elton had been formed a year previously as we were recording *Make It Big* in 1984. While working at Château Miraval, a recording studio in Correns in the south of France, George and I received a call from our management company in London. Apparently, an unexpected invitation had reached their desk.

'Er, George, Andrew: Elton John has been in touch. He'd like to know if you fancied joining him for lunch?'

We were both taken aback. *Bloody hell! Lunch with Elton John?* The idea seemed surreal and we couldn't believe our luck. A few days later, and feeling a little nervous, we drove over to meet our host, who was immediately charming, big-hearted and very kind to both of us as we started an afternoon of drinking and eating. Both of us had heard tales of the legendary opulence of Elton's hospitality, and as two boys from Bushey, then only twenty-one years old, it was quite an intimidating experience. The wit at the table was rapid-fire; it could be acerbic too, with Elton holding court from one end of a lavish feast in the elegant surroundings of his sunny patio. But everything was done to make us feel welcome, and as the wine flowed I realised any anxiety we'd felt in advance of the gathering had been far more unsettling than the event itself. We shared stories and told jokes. The mood was so relaxed and natural that, at times, I had to remind myself of our host's enormous reputation.

Good times were such that lunch ran into evening, and our group moved on to a nearby nightclub where Elton's songwriting partner, Bernie Taupin, joined the party. By that stage, all of us were fairly well oiled. Somebody mentioned that the actress Joan Collins had moored her yacht in Saint-Tropez's harbour. Leaving the party, and fuelled by alcohol and the memories of her somewhat racy film *The Stud* – in which she'd played a nymphomaniac nightclub owner – George shouted across the water, 'Joan! Show us your knickers!' It was an uncharacteristically lowbrow outburst.

It felt entirely fitting that two years later another

Backstage with Elton, Wembley Stadium, 28 June 1986

Wham! party was drawing to a close with Elton alongside us for the ride. 'Young Guns (Go For It!)', our first hit, and 'Wake Me Up Before You Go-Go', George's incomparable call to the dance floor, was followed by an anarchic encore of 'I'm Your Man', with Duran Duran's Simon Le Bon joining us onstage for backing vocals. As the music faded out, the din of seventy-two thousand voices echoing around us, we enjoyed the clamour together one last time. The two of us had shared experiences that were unimaginable when we'd first left school. Ever since that day, we had been reliant upon each other.

In that regard, Wembley was both brilliant and bittersweet. Part of me was happy to escape the limelight that accompanied life in a stadium-sized pop band. I was tired of the circus that surrounded Wham! at all times. The hype and hysteria had become too much and my relationship with the national press was hostile. Saying goodbye to the tumult and the palaver that surrounded George and myself wasn't a hardship, but the knowledge that we'd not perform alongside one another as Wham! again was tinged with melancholy. We had grown up together and this sense of union had pulled us even closer to the hearts of our fans. We were an inseparably tight-knit duo – *a brotherhood*. But that friendship wasn't without its lows at times.

My best friend was really one of two people throughout our close relationship – before Wham! and after.

The schoolboy I'd first met as a thirteen-year-old who would go on to be my best friend, the boy I'd wanted by my side during those first strides towards musical superstardom and beyond, became George Michael, the character he created to propel his career from singer in a number 1 pop duo to a solo star brimming with ambition and creative wanderlust. By the time of that final concert the second incarnation was well on its way to completion. George shot to even greater stardom when he released *Faith* in 1987. But he was beset by confusion, a consequence of his sexuality and the struggles to define the reality beneath his public image. The tension only seemed to play out more publicly later on.

Throughout Wham! and beyond, the bond between us was both real and heartfelt. The British public seemed to find our easy relationship a joyful thing during a period of British history that is now recalled as being pretty tough. We had first arrived with 'Wham Rap (Enjoy What You Do)', an antidote to the despondency of unemployment with its lyrics:

> Wham! Bam!
> I am! A man!
> Job or no job,
> You can't tell me that I'm not.

From then on, our music became a soundtrack to the country's newfound optimism and self-confidence.

Songs such as 'Club Tropicana', 'Wake Me Up Before You Go-Go', 'Freedom' and 'I'm Your Man' embodied excitement and aspiration. Everything looked effortlessly fun for us because it *was* effortlessly fun, and that natural exuberance translated into huge commercial success. The early demos that George and I recorded in my parents' front room nudged us towards a record deal and eventually sales of over thirty million records. Our debut album *Fantastic* went to number 1 in 1983. Its follow-up, *Make It Big*, repeated the achievement on a global scale a year later. We sold out stadium shows in Britain and America, drawing fans to our music until Whamania became a global phenomenon.

Our union drew to a close in 1986, in part because Wham! was unable to outlive our youth. Continuing to distil the very essence of teenage emotion once we grew up was a pop alchemy beyond even George's prodigious songwriting talents. Meanwhile, during the first flush of success and before the release of *Fantastic*, we'd decided that Wham!'s creative reins should rest solely with George if we were to achieve the scale of success we believed was in our reach. I had long recognised his ability, and my sole ambition had been simply to be in a band and play music, so I was satisfied with just being in the studio, or onstage. The decision still smarted a little, but it was the right one: George was so clearly developing into a writer of rare ability; indeed it was the desire to realise the potential of that gift which

drove him to become a solo artist, free of our band's constraints. Now, after four thrilling years, our time together was over.

George shouted in my ear. From within the noise and the chaos I wasn't able to catch any words. Our musicians and backing singers, most of them long-term collaborators, had left the stage to allow us our last moments together as Wham!. The Wembley crowd was swaying ever faster, singing even louder in a sea of sound and colour; banners and flags dotted the view ahead.

'*What?* Come again!' I yelled over the din, sensing that what he had to say was important.

George smiled and embraced me, resting his head upon my shoulder one last time before we took our final bows.

'I couldn't have done this without you, Andy,' he said.

PART ONE
Young Guns

1. Decisions, Decisions

November 1979

We were the best of friends, and two sides of the same coin. Georgios Panayiotou was a studious and shy, broccoli-haired sixteen-year-old with a muffin-top waistline and a wardrobe full of questionable outfits. I, on the other hand, was self-assured and outgoing. A bright spark, but not so clever; a smart alec mischief-maker dressed in a charity-shop mohair suit and parka jacket, swerving studies for my A-levels in a school that had bored me to tears. But the pair of us were joined at the hip through a shared love of music, *Monty Python* sketches and our juvenile humour. And then I made the decision that would change both our lives forever.

Yog, we're forming a band . . .

For the best part of two years, it had been all I'd thought about, and having spent so much time in each other's pockets at school, there was only one person I wanted to play music with: the boy set to become

George Michael. He had great rhythm and feel, an out-
standing sense of melody and he was an even better
singer. During our early friendship we'd idolised the
same bands and artists, a wide variety of music from
favourites like Queen to new sounds from the likes of
Manchester's Joy Division. By 1979, we were into ska, a
very modern British take on reggae that mixed Carib-
bean grooves with jagged guitars. Bands such as The
Specials, Madness, The Beat and Steel Pulse had captured our imaginations, not just musically but through
their clothes, too. With a mod revival also under way following the release of the movie *Quadrophenia*, kids across
England were suddenly dressing in sharp suits and Hush
Puppies shoes. Buzz cuts were a cool choice at the hair-
dresser's. Luckily my life in suburban Hertfordshire was
as tuned in to the scene as the kids clubbing in London
or Birmingham. *Music was something I wanted to be a part of.*

'But, Andy,' said Yog when I called him after school,
'I want to, but I can't . . .'

There were some mumbled excuses about A-level
pressure and the unforgiving mood of his parents,
who seemed eager to protect him from any further
distractions – like me. However, I wasn't about to be
deterred. I'd set my heart on this course of action and
I wasn't about to let Yog's concerns about his mum and
dad thwart it.

'No, it's now or never,' I told him. 'We're forming a
band today.'

Yog knew I could be single minded, especially once my mind was set on something. He also understood that I wasn't actually asking him, *I was telling him.* Sensing that I wasn't about to give up, his resistance fizzled away.

'OK, Andy,' he said, taking a deep breath. 'Let's do it.'

Yog was in. Now I had something to be excited about, a goal to achieve – *a purpose.* As far as I was concerned, there was nothing we couldn't do and nobody that would stand in our way. Our friendship was invincible, and to my mind chart success awaited. I had no idea what that success would actually mean, but I could feel it. *I knew it.* What eventually took place was more spectacular than I could ever have imagined . . .

2. The New Boy

I first set eyes on Georgios Panayiotou while waiting for the first lesson of the new school year to start. Around me, the other kids of form 2A1 at Bushey Meads Comprehensive chatted excitedly. Boys bragged of snogging sessions with mysterious girls while on holiday with their parents, usually at British seaside resorts. (To go abroad in those days as a family was a financial luxury beyond most people.) Girls giggled and swooned over picture pull-outs of David Essex and Donny Osmond taken from the pages of *Jackie* magazine. Everybody seemed more fascinated by Pan's People than ever before. The dance troupe from *Top of the Pops* had been performing on the show for several years, but the Lycra-clad dancers were fast becoming the stuff of young boys' dreams and everyone had a favourite. But after six weeks of summer freedom I couldn't find my usual enthusiasm for the noisy buzz of the first day back.

Age Group 10-11 Years   Class 4W

Report for Autumn Term 1973   Name ANDREW RIDGELEY

	GRADE
MATHEMATICS	B-
ENGLISH : Expression : Written	B
Oral	B+
Reading	A-
GENERAL SUBJECTS : History, Geography, Science	B-
HANDWRITING	B+
ART AND CRAFT	B
MUSIC	B
RELIGIOUS EDUCATION	B-
PHYSICAL EDUCATION	B-
Conduct Disruptive.	
Absences	4

NOTE: A,B,C,D,E in "Grade" column denotes that the standard
of work is Very Good, Good, Average, Weak or Very Weak,
in the appropriate AGE GROUP

Andrew has achieved some good results which might be
even better if he applied himself more than he does. In Maths
his work does not always match his capabilities. In English his
written work is always interesting ; he writes imaginative stories and poems.
He has let himself down in General Subjects by not completing all
the work to be done. The work completed has, however, been of a good standard. His
Art work shows good imagination but again he doesn't always finish. He
tries hard in PE/Games and in music (although he no longer plays his
recorder). Andrew has a good speaking voice but unfortunately he uses it at the
wrong times as well as the right.

Teacher R Swebato   Headmaster E. Halliwell

The next term starts on Tuesday, 8th January 1974.

I was bored.

In fact I was often bored. To my mind, school was a drag and once I'd learned how to read and write, cruising through primary school with barely a hiccup, my participation in the British educational system was effectively at an end. Any interest in my academic career all but disappeared from that point on and I really couldn't see the relevance of lessons, which annoyed both my teachers and parents. One school report cited me as 'disruptive' and a succession of parents' evenings – and the inevitable dressing-downs in their fallout – became a chastening experience. One of the few things I enjoyed about it was playing for the school football team. But contrary to a later claim by George, I never harboured any hopes of becoming a professional footballer. I supported Manchester United and that was as far as my ambitions ever went.

And so I was placed class front, from where my teachers could keep an eye on any misdemeanours. I was twelve years old and prickly about authority. With my top button undone and school tie loosened just so, I looked every bit the sullen, difficult teen, which might have accounted for one or two teachers taking a dim view of me. I was hardly a complete delinquent, however. Although form 2A1 was considered the brightest in the year, given none of us had done well enough in our 11-plus test to go to any of Watford's grammar schools, it was unlikely that we were destined for careers in nuclear physics or neuroscience.

There was a sudden change in mood in the classroom. Conversations regarding Pan's People, David Essex and those awkward summer kisses were shushed when our form tutor, Mrs Parker, entered the room, trailed by a nervous-looking boy. Dressed in a pristine, box-fresh school uniform, he wore a pair of oversized steel-framed specs. His hair, which looked like a dressing-up wig, appeared to have been made from coarse man-made fibre. And the pressure of facing down a room of new classmates had clearly shaken him. As Mrs Parker welcomed the New Kid to form 2A1, he began to redden. A clumsy introduction where his name was delivered with all the finesse of an urban fox tearing open a bin liner didn't help.

'Boys and girls, this is your new classmate, Yor-rioss Paneyeottoo,' she said, pronouncing his name phonetically. She looked down at the horrified face at her side for assistance, but the new boy – *whatever his name was* – had now blushed the colour of a strawberry Opal Fruit. The girls in the front row giggled; boys sniggered from the back of the class. But undeterred and keen to press ahead with her morning, Mrs Parker continued with the formalities, though any attempt to repeat the unfamiliar Mediterranean name was abandoned.

'OK, I'd like someone to take care of the new boy,'

she said. 'Someone sensible please, to act as a mentor and to show him around during his first week or so. This is an important responsibility, so whoever assumes the role will have to make our new addition feel welcome at Bushey Meads. Who'd like to help?'

There was an awkward pause. My classmates were hesitating and I couldn't figure out why. I had never been given a new boy before and this was an opportunity too good to miss: a welcome diversion from the monotony of lessons. I shot my hand into the air. I couldn't tell whether or not Mrs Parker was pleased because although she was smiling, it was in a way that suggested she wasn't about to be taken for a bloody idiot. Her arched eyebrow also delivered a firm warning not to cock things up.

'Thank you, Andrew, that's very kind,' she said eventually, gesturing to *Whatshisface* that we should sit together for the school register. With Mrs Parker running through the list of names, all eyes were on the New Boy as he edged nervously towards me. I couldn't help but feel a little sorry for him.

'Adams.'

'Yes, miss.'

'Bartlett.'

'Yes, miss.'

'Brown.'

'Yes, miss.'

'The name's a bit tricky at first, I know,' he said,

sitting alongside me. 'It's Greek,' he added, sensing my confusion.

I shrugged and nodded sympathetically. With a name like Georgios, I knew the New Boy was in for a choppy first term. But as we chatted, I learned some key facts about Bushey Meads's latest face. Georgios's dad owned his own restaurant. The family had previously lived in Kingsbury, London, before relocating to nearby Radlett, which, while not being as close to the school gates as my parents' house, was still near enough for the possibility of after-school misadventures, should we hit it off. I also sensed that Georgios's family might be quite wealthy; Radlett was considered to be very well heeled. But just as things seemed to be running smoothly, the pair of us struck a conversational pothole. He didn't appear to share any of my interests and there was no love for football and even less enthusiasm for Formula One. We looked at each other in a pause that threatened to become an uncomfortable silence. When I glanced up, Mrs Parker was staring at me sceptically.

Bloody hell, this was not going well.

And then, just as I began to feel I'd made an almighty blunder in taking on such a responsibility, I made a breakthrough.

'So, what music are you into?' I asked.

Georgios was now smiling. *Success!* I'd obviously found some common ground. He liked Queen, he said, which was a great start as far as I was concerned. And while form 2A1 worked through all the boring tasks required at the beginning of every school year, the pair of us chatted about Freddie Mercury, the blazing guitars of Brian May and 'Killer Queen', the song released about a year earlier that had redefined the band's sound. Just as reassuring was Georgios's love for the Beatles and David Bowie. By the time we'd stumbled across a shared love of Elton John, our worlds were undoubtedly aligning and we walked from registration to our first class throwing our favourite songs back and forth. 'Benny And The Jets', 'Candle In The Wind' and the title track from his most recent album, *Goodbye Yellow Brick Road*, were all personal favourites. We sat down for our first French lesson still talking about music. But I was distracted, miles away, and within moments of the class starting I'd been ticked off for not paying enough attention.

'Ridgeley, how about we start this year the right way?' said a grumpy teacher, which suggested my card had been marked yet again.

When I looked across at Georgios, he was laughing, rolling his eyes in support. He seems all right, this fella, I thought. Maybe the year isn't going to be so bad after all . . .

Less than an hour into the new school year and I had a new mate.

*

Georgios explained that the best way to say his name was Yor-goh, which sounded like hawking up a particularly unpleasant glop of phlegm. Somewhat inevitably, this was then twisted into Yoghurt, but to my surprise the nickname didn't seem to get much of a reaction. I eventually settled into calling him Yog, which was so much easier than his given name. Mrs Parker's vague stab at the Greek pronunciation was depressingly matched by her colleagues' until, one by one, they all seemed to give up, calling him George until everybody but his closest friends followed suit. When it came to being introduced to new faces, it was the name Georgios preferred to go by, probably because it took the shortest of explanations.

Over the next few days I learned more and more about my new best friend. Top of the list was that he was fairly determined when he needed to be, which belied my first impression of him being a shy and insecure teenager. Yog quickly settled into life at Bushey Meads.

During his first lunch break I showed him the ropes in a popular game called King of the Wall. It was just as the name suggested, and the rules were fairly basic. One kid clambered to the top of a wall, only for his or her rivals to try to knock them from their perch by any means necessary. No regulations, no referees and no quarter given.

That afternoon, I used those slightly above average

Pele✓ Cruyff✓ Robson✓ Ridgeley✗

With cousin Martin and a disc recognising lots
of single sales.

PE skills to take the concrete throne. *I was King of the Wall.* Taunting my friends, I shoved aside a few contenders before being caught off guard. It was Yog. Tired of the peacocking, he'd decided to knock me off balance with a shove in the back. I fell to the asphalt below and then suffered the embarrassment of seeing him as he swaggered along the top of the wall, laughing at his own bravado. Yog might not have worn his strength as visible armour, and he hadn't proved much use on the football pitch, then the playground barometer for physical prowess, but I could tell he wasn't about to be cowed by anybody.

A week later, my suspicions that Yog's family might be fairly well off were confirmed when I was invited to his house. Together we rode on the school bus to Radlett. I was impressed by the four-bedroomed detached house with its large garden and fancy patio. It was a far cry from Mum and Dad's three-bedroomed semi. In contrast to our modest but well-tended flowerbeds, Yog's home had a large lawn that sloped gently up from the patio area at the back of the house. During the summer evenings, the Panayiotous would dine al fresco on Mediterranean culinary delicacies including dolmades, hummus and taramasalata. It all seemed pretty exotic compared to the more traditional fare on offer back home.

After saying hello to his parents we went upstairs to Yog's bedroom. It was immaculately tidy and a treasure chest of cool memorabilia and musical equipment. Mine, by contrast, was an anarchic jumble of clothes and magazines that was only ever tidied under my parents' threat of a trip to the local rubbish tip. Yog had posters of stars like David Bowie and Elton John across his walls. Most surprising, however, was the fact that Yog collected *Spider-Man* comics. He owned a stack of them, one of which was the very first edition – a highly prized possession even then. Yog told me that he'd seen Elton John live at Watford FC's Vicarage Road ground a year earlier and that he had only been to one football match, at Arsenal. But as he showed me his stereo, my attention was already elsewhere: at the end of the bed was a sodding great pearlescent-blue drum kit. I couldn't believe it. While Yog's drums weren't of the scale used by the likes of Phil Collins or Queen's Roger Taylor, I was blown away. Nobody I knew had a drum kit in their bedroom and before he'd had time to protest I made for the seat and thrashed out a heavy, ear-splitting four-four rhythm on the snare, two toms, bass drum and high hat.

'No, Andrew . . . *don't!*' shouted Yog over the din.

I had upset him and the horrified look on his face told me I'd overstepped the mark. I later learned that in the Panayiotou household, music practice was only permitted at certain times of the day and I'd been way off. A little taken aback, I moved away from the drum kit and switched my enthusiasm to the stereo standing in one corner of the room.

'I always record the Top 40 on Sunday afternoons,' he explained. 'I keep the songs I like . . .'

My mum only had a portable cassette recorder, whereas Yog had a double tape deck that he could record onto directly from the tuner. This was quite an upgrade. We were both keen chart fans, but like me he found the tone set by DJs on Radio 1 and Capital Radio tried his patience. The hyperbole and matey chatter of DJs like Dave Lee Travis and Tony Blackburn made us cringe. This new connection inspired us to record a few pastiche jingles and conversational pieces of our own. For an hour we beavered away at Yog's tape deck, mocking the radio personalities that seemed most ridiculous to us. Though unaware of it at the time, we were creating our own little bubble, defining the landscape of a closely woven friendship: music and comedy. We ad-libbed sketches, bounced ideas off one another and poked fun at an adult world that seemed to take itself too seriously. The sound of our messing around probably alarmed and reassured Yog's mum in equal measure.

Throughout the evening we flicked through what was a brilliant record collection. Yog owned music by a lot of the artists I loved, including albums from Queen. While I liked Bowie and had a number of singles, 'The Jean Genie' among them, Yog was a keen fan and he'd collected several LPs. Elton John was an entirely different matter, though. Both Yog and I loved

38

him because he was a great songwriter. He could write in such varied styles that singles such as 'Crocodile Rock' and 'Candle In The Wind' were totally different in sound. I was a bit too young to have been aware of his first few albums, but from *Goodbye Yellow Brick Road* onwards, I became an avid fan and soon bought *Madman Across The Water, Honky Chateau* and *Don't Shoot Me I'm Only The Piano Player*. It was Elton's gift that his music was a perfect expression of the lyrics written by Bernie Taupin, especially in 'Candle In The Wind'. Bernie had the words and Elton relayed their emotions through melody. They did it better than anyone else.

We loved Elton's persona. The idea of this character playing the piano in crazy sunglasses and a pair of oversized platform boots was fascinating. David Bowie was similarly intriguing. Both artists seemed larger than life. Their carefully constructed images were all-important and we both loved the outrageous nature of those singers, as we did Freddie Mercury. With his catsuits, glorious hair and flamboyant posturing, Queen's frontman was a charismatic artist who had been impossible to ignore. All three had changed their names – another fact not lost on Yog.

Yog had heavier and more eclectic tastes, too. When a family friend gave him Led Zeppelin's entire back catalogue, we instantly thought the band was amazing – we couldn't believe we'd missed out on them and soon got into 'Whole Lotta Love', 'Kashmir' and 'When

The Levee Breaks'. It was exciting to retrospectively discover a groundbreaking band and then binge on their whole back catalogue. Later in life, George gave the impression he'd been raised solely on a musical portfolio of David Bowie, Stevie Wonder and a raft of Motown artists. While those records were certainly somewhere in that collection, it was actually far broader than people were led to believe. That evening, as we listened to some of his favourite albums, dissecting the lyrics and sleeve notes printed inside, I found it amazing to know there was somebody else as completely absorbed by music as I was.

It was soon time for home and when I left, Lesley, Yog's mum, was friendly, but noticeably unsure of me at the same time. Despite my best efforts, she wasn't taking to me in the same way that my other friends' parents had in the past, and judging by her reaction as I waved goodbye from my mum's car, I had the distinct feeling she had some reservations about her son's self-confident new friend. I couldn't remember doing or saying anything that might have upset her; I'd only spent the evening being myself. (Which might have been enough to do the trick, I suppose.) I wasn't too fussed, though, and as far as I was concerned my first trip to Yog's house had been a great laugh.

Everything was going just swimmingly.

3. Parallel Lines

Lesley's concerns for Yog were understandable, but given the Panayiotous' determined attitude, the chances of her son coming off the rails were slim. His dad, Jack, was a positive role model: a grafter and a self-made man. His real name was Kyriacos Panayiotou and he'd moved to Britain during the 1950s when tensions between the Turkish and Greek populations in northeast Cyprus had boiled over into bloody violence. After escaping to London, Kyriacos used the anglicized version of his Christian name and shortened his surname to Panos; then he displayed a work ethic that would define his life. He worked all hours to make ends meet.

When Jack later married Lesley, whom he'd met in London, he went on to open his own restaurant in Edgware. Jack was still working incredibly hard when I first came to meet Yog. He was rarely at home, but his presence was always felt whenever he could spend time with the family. Although he was a man of few words, on the occasions that Jack did speak to me he was gruff and to the point; at times bordering on the intimidating. He also considered me a negative influence on his son. When Yog's dad was in the house I usually tried not to be too conspicuous, but I later grew to be very fond of Lesley, despite any reservations she might have had about her son's friendship with me. She was a lovely woman.

There was at least one similarity between Yog's background and mine. Both of us were kids of immigrant fathers. My dad was born Albert Mario Zacharia in Alexandria, Egypt, in 1933, where he was the son of an Italian mother and an Egyptian father of Yemeni descent. Egypt was under British rule at the time and Alexandria was a cultural melting pot. My father grew up speaking a number of languages. English was no problem, as that was the language he spoke at home with his brother, and so he settled in easily at the British Boys' School in Alexandria. Passing his exams, he eventually became a student teacher at the same school. However, trouble was brewing. When the Suez Crisis erupted in 1956, my father's family was expelled from Egypt amid a surge of nationalism and they relocated to Essex. Like Jack, Dad's family had been forced to leave their home during a time of conflict. In the mid 1950s, National Service was still mandatory. After discovering Dad was fluent in a number of languages, the RAF sent him to St Andrew's University in Scotland to read Russian and German in anticipation of a role with the RAF in Cold War Berlin.

The discrimination experienced by his family in Egypt was so unpleasant that my father became keen to integrate into his new home. Before being sent to St Andrew's with the R A F, he was on the bus when he saw on a street sign *Ridgeley Gardens.* That's a very English-sounding name, he thought. And Zacharia might put me at a disadvantage, so . . . The name stuck and Albert Ridgeley, who was fluent in Arabic, German, Russian, French and Italian, followed St Andrew's with the Joint Services School for Linguists, before being posted to Berlin as an interpreter in Air Force intelligence. Despite his multicultural roots, however, Dad felt immediately British – as did I. While I was growing up, it was obvious to me that I was a little darker-skinned than most of my friends, while being part of the same culture: as English as Wimbledon's Tennis Championships, or bacon and eggs; whereas Yog's family seemed more attached to their Cypriot history. Unlike my dad, who sounded thoroughly English, Jack's accent was still very strong.

My parents met when Dad eventually left the R A F in 1960, taking a job in a camera shop, which he enjoyed given he was also a keen amateur photographer. He met my mum, Jennifer Dunlop, when she was just eighteen and still at school. Despite her age, she was strong-willed and independent and they fell in love. When she became pregnant Dad married her out of a sense of honour and duty. I – the cause of their hastily arranged wedding – arrived in January 1963 and

What a jolly little fellow!

Shotgun wedding, Home Counties style. Albert Ridgeley and his new wife Jennifer, circa summer 1962.

My grandpa, John Frederick Dunlop, and an infant Andrew Ridgeley.
A wonderful, loving man. And he always made me laugh – lots!

On holiday in Devon, circa 1972. When the sun always
shone in the summer!

Paul Ridgeley came along in February 1964, but it was only on the day of their twenty-fifth wedding anniversary that I realised Mum had been three months pregnant when she'd tied the knot with Dad in 1962. A mini-scandal had been averted.

Life for the Ridgeley family was initially played out in a small house in a suburban council estate in Egham. The modest home was filled with the voices of Mum, Dad and two small boys, plus my paternal grandfather who, at times, seemed to have been transported from another world entirely. My brother and I were oblivious to his life and the traumas inflicted upon him during the Second World War and called him 'Drac' because of his unsmiling demeanour and resemblance to Count Dracula. Granddad drank can after can of Coca-Cola and smoked like a chimney. In 1968 we moved to a 1930s semi-detached house at 40 Ashfield Avenue in Bushey, but Granddad stayed behind in Egham until, a few years later, the cigarettes finally finished him off.

Once Paul and I had both started at infants' school, Mum had the opportunity to pursue a career and she enrolled at Wall Hall Teacher Training College. The old neo-Gothic building had an outdoor swimming pool and Mum used to take us there every now and again on warm days. I loved messing about in the water. But as I grew into my teens and was allowed to hang around at the down-at-heel King George V Recreation Ground in Bushey, it soon became the main focus for my social life, thanks mainly to its football pitch, tennis courts and café. But the pool there proved to be its biggest draw. After school I'd hurry home, grab my Speedos and dash to the Rec, which to my mind became an aquatic wonder-world. I spent hours perfecting different types of bombs, a type of jump into the water, designed to create a massive splash, giving them names like the Preacher, the Can Opener and the Nutcracker, each one executed in order to soak the sunbathing girls nearby. Between Wall Hall and the Rec, the seventies felt like a succession of endless summers.

As primary school kids, both Paul and I understood we'd better play nicely, *or else*. Mum was quite handy with a wooden spoon and when her patience had been stretched to breaking point would chase us around the garden whacking our backsides as she went. I don't recall being a particularly naughty boy, but I was certainly a little wayward at times and very inquisitive. So, when my parents hosted a party one weekend, I got up early the next morning, hoping to discover exactly what the grown-ups had been up to during the night before. I was only seven years old, and with my parents enjoying a rare Sunday lie-in I coerced my little brother into joining me. The pair of us crept downstairs to explore.

First we came across an open tin of Watney's Party Seven beer, a prerequisite of any 1970s gathering. We each took a swig before spitting it straight back out because it was so disgusting. Undeterred, we then opened Mum's hand-carved wooden box, which was always filled with cigarettes and used only on special occasions. Grabbing a ciggy each and a box of matches, we snuck into the back yard and lit up, puffing away like the grown-ups, while coughing and spluttering. We immediately gave up on our adventure, hiding the evidence in a dustbin.

But we had been spotted.

Mr Smith, our nosy-parker neighbour, had seen it all and took great pleasure telling Mum, who delivered the ultimate sanction: *Wait 'til your father gets home.* The next few hours were spent in fear awaiting the inevitable punishment. When the time arrived, we were called downstairs and given the mother and father of all tongue-lashings. Dad then spanked us all the way to bed without any tea. I'm not sure the punishment fitted the crime, but it certainly worked. I've never let a Watney's beer pass my lips since.

Part of my father's upbringing influenced me greatly when I was little. Given his military background, Dad was fascinated by the Second World War and collected a series of magazines detailing its history. Whenever they arrived in the post I'd read them from cover to cover and I can still identify fighter planes from that era simply from their silhouettes. My interest later extended to making Airfix model kits, and as a twelve-year-old I often blew my entire paper-round wages on

A de Havilland DH 106 Comet, a Hawker Hurricane, and two small boys.

Albert Ridgeley, lead side drummer. Somewhere in Germany, late 1950s.

model planes, tanks and ships, plus the all-important glue and paint.

I was lucky to have any money, as I was probably the world's worst paperboy: indolent, feckless and prone to loitering. I was so easily distracted that, at weekends, the papers were usually delivered around lunchtime. Customers complained. People left their houses to search for me. They had every right to be ticked off, especially the lady who found me drinking the Baby-cham she'd left in her garage one Sunday morning. I was caught red-handed and sent away in shame. Unsur-prisingly enough, I later got the sack.

Dad's other big influence was much more significant – *music*.

Dad had been the lead side drummer in an RAF military band and he and Mum were keen that we boys learn an instrument so I took keyboard lessons from the age of seven. We had a stand-up piano I practised on at home. I soon realised that as well as playing the pieces from the instruction books my teacher had given me, I loved composing music. In fact, I enjoyed coming up with my own melodies more than playing. I just saw the piano as a tool for the job. Perhaps it's no surprise that I later gave up the lessons. I only went back to the instrument in my teens when, fuelled by a new passion for music, I wanted to write songs again. Those early lessons must have paid off, though.

Dad's pride and joy was a stereo in our dining room and he preferred to listen to records using a pair of expensive Sennheiser headphones. During those rare, quiet moments in a house overrun with two young boys, he'd put on his headphones and sit back, close his eyes and lose himself in the music. But during Sunday evenings the whole family gathered round the speakers for the Top 40 countdown. There was no joking, dancing or messing around, though. We perched on the vinyl-covered sofa with our tea, listening to the likes of Sweet, Slade and Alvin Stardust in a weekly ritual that shaped my love for pop and rock'n'roll and planted the idea of music as a life-affirming force.

While our record collection might have been limited, it was certainly influential. I flicked through my mum and dad's LPs over and over, playing records by the Beatles, the Everly Brothers and a Rolling Stones compilation called *Big Hits (High Tide And Green Grass)* which featured all the early singles like 'Paint It Black', 'It's All Over Now', '(I Can't Get No) Satisfaction' and 'Get Off Of My Cloud'. The Stones sounded raw, visceral; everything about them was exhilarating, but they struggled for my affections against personal favourites like the Beatles' *Help!* and a compilation called *Twenty-Five Rock'n'Roll Greats*, which featured songs like Little Richard's 'Tutti Frutti', 'Rock Around The Clock' by Bill Haley and the Comets and 'Hound Dog' by Elvis. With the volume turned up, I'd twist and jive around the front room, but only if I was sure nobody else was home. When I heard the front door slam, I'd leap for the record player, then sit down quickly while pretending not to be out of breath. The embarrassment of being discovered mid twist would have been crushing.

I can't recall the first single or album picked up for my collection, but looking through racks of vinyl in search of something to spend my pocket money on soon became an adventure. Elton John's *Goodbye Yellow Brick Road* was one of my first memorable discoveries. I'd bought it after it was played non-stop by our coach driver on his cutting-edge eight track tape player for the duration of a school trip journey to the Wye valley, and its cover made it even more special. It arrived as a gatefold, and each set of song lyrics printed inside was accompanied by an illustration. The pictures were brilliant: Marilyn Monroe for 'Candle In The Wind', a pistol for 'Roy Rogers' and a dragon accompanying 'Grey Seal'. Elton's *Captain Fantastic And The Brown Dirt Cowboy* was even more lavish and included three or four pullouts, one of which was a lyric booklet, and another a cartoon picture book. I later learned that one version of the cover even had a pop-up design.

Yog and I often went record shopping together and I have a distinct memory of the pair of us poring over the sleeve of the Electric Light Orchestra's 1977 album *Out Of The Blue*, which included their big hit 'Mr Blue Sky', while waiting for a train at Golders Green station.

As kids, he and I were both really into the design of record sleeves and I spent ages studying incredible covers, such as *Tales From Topographic Oceans* by prog rock band Yes. While I never bought any albums purely because of their design, it was possible to appreciate the surreal art whether you liked the music or not. Luckily some of my favourite bands combined visual flair with great songs, and when I became a fan of Genesis – through either *The Old Grey Whistle Test* on BBC Two, or my friend Roy, who had pretty esoteric music tastes: Gong, Genesis and Captain Beefheart were among his favourites. I was delighted when Genesis' *Wind And Wuthering* album was released in 1976 with an embossed logo on the card front, an effect that gave the sleeve an unusual texture. The music inside was just as good.

It wasn't long before I was seeing my favourite bands for real, and my first gig proved unforgettable. When Queen played Earls Court in 1977 I went with Roy who had tickets and was blown away by Freddie Mercury, despite being about as far away from the stage as was possible. I was lucky enough to see them again at Alexandra Palace two years later when Yog and I bought tickets. I was transfixed by Freddie Mercury. He had dressed for the occasion in a harlequin catsuit. The band played through their big hits – 'Crazy Little Thing Called Love', 'Fat Bottomed Girls', 'Bicycle Race' – and while Brian May's unique guitar-playing sounded incredible, Freddie dominated the performance with an energy I've never seen in a singer since, not even Prince.

Genesis were just as good and I went to see them with Yog at Earls Court in 1977, turning up on the night to buy tickets at the door. Amazingly, our seats were only three rows from the front and the stage looked spectacular. Glowing vari-lights, which were a new development back then, hung from the ceiling to create a series of ethereal white stalactites. This was another transitional period for Genesis and their style was becoming more mainstream. With Peter Gabriel's departure they'd become noticeably less left-field, and they were now, with albums like *A Trick Of The Tail* and *Wind And Wuthering*, developing into something we both found more appealing. I loved watching Phil Collins perform; to drum with the energy and style that he did while singing at the same time was unbelievable. The following year, we went to see them again, this time at Knebworth. It was a great show, but we were stuck 400 metres away from the stage and it couldn't hope to match the intensity of that memorable night at Earls Court.

Whenever I played my Genesis or Queen records at home, I always took great care. Dad's stereo was a treasured possession every bit as valuable as the car, or Mum's wedding ring. Money was always tight. We rarely redecorated the house and costly holidays were a luxury that was beyond us, but the stereo was Dad's big-ticket item and one of the few possessions in the house that was very much *his*. It was a real privilege for us to use it. As my own musical tastes evolved we were still gathering around it to listen to the Top 40. That pleasure, though, paled in comparison to Thursday evenings. At seven thirty, it seemed as if the whole nation gathered around their TVs to watch *Top of the Pops*. BBC One's flagship music show was a must-see event for anyone with a passing interest in pop during the 1970s and would be for a few decades to come. Both the Ridgeley and Panayiotou families watched the show avidly.

For *Top of the Pops*'s viewers, the likes of T. Rex, the New Seekers and ABBA were big draws. Queen grabbed me with their *Top of the Pops* performance of 'Killer Queen', but Blondie grabbed *everybody* on a damp February evening in 1978, thanks to the appearance of lead singer Debbie Harry, who was a riot of sexuality in nothing more than an oversized red shirt and thigh-length boots. The next morning in school, Blondie was the only topic worth discussing. And Debbie Harry represented a subject that was going to loom large in my youth. I was beginning to understand the power of the Pop Star.

4. Teenage Kicks

Any self-respecting teen of the mid 1970s knew that the right look was essential to their friends' respect, not to mention his or her romantic prospects. I was no exception. Long before Wham! made it big, I developed a taste for eyecatching clothes and put together a distinctive wardrobe that reflected my outgoing personality.

At the age of thirteen that meant high street fashion in Watford, our nearest shopping centre. But fortnightly visits with Mum and Paul eventually turned into solo sweeps of Watford Market. These trips ushered in a lifetime of interesting clothing choices, not to mention one or two regrettable outfits to match one or two regrettable hairstyles. Shopping excursions to Watford were something to look forward to. The streets were busy and thriving, especially near the bottom of the high street where I would linger by the coffee roaster's shop to inhale the wonderful aromas wafting from inside. It was a little oasis of individuality on a parade of otherwise familiar names like Woolworth's, Our Price and Safeway.

Anyone with an eye on fashion knew to avoid the main drag and visit the nearby market in search of the latest must-have designs. It was here that that I made my first major fashion faux pas: a pair of needlecord trousers in a gaudy shade of bottle green with a high waistband and four buttons. Stuffing my hands into the deep pockets made me look like a hunchback. Not that I was bothered in the slightest. All my friends looked similarly idiotic. Matching the trousers with a pair of platform boots, we thought we were the coolest things in Bushey.

Some purchases were more extravagant than others. I'd saved up £8, a small fortune in 1975, for a pair of oxblood-red rockers. Whenever an important date appeared in my social calendar I'd put them on, hoping to impress my mates, or any girls I might meet. Within six months they were out of fashion.

In my own mind at least, carrying it all off posed few problems: I was brimming with self-confidence. Where that came from, I can't be sure exactly, but my home environment probably played a part. My mother had me when she was just eighteen and later went on to become a teacher; she was somebody who was clearly capable of dealing with whatever life threw at her and getting on with it, and some of that must have rubbed off on me. Overall, though, my confidence was allowed to flourish at home and I wasn't held back in any way. Both my brother and myself were allowed to express ourselves

Me sporting a 'wet look' jacket. Probably going to get a lot wetter-looking soon judging by Paul's kagool!

however we wanted (within reason), whether that was model-making, playing football, music or anything else. And while it was always clear that my dad thought academic success was important, there was no real pressure.

I'm not sure it was quite the same for Yog. His father was a very strong character and seemed to have a very narrow view of how life should be led and what his son needed to do to be a success. That Yog was perhaps a more sensitive boy than I was would only have exacerbated the effect of that. As I became older, looks also began to play a bigger part in the development of my self-esteem. While I didn't think I was a particularly good-looking kid, I wouldn't have regarded myself as being ugly either. But once girls started to notice me, aged seventeen or eighteen, my self-belief increased. I'd also always gleaned confidence from the way people treated me: I'd been taught to be polite and considerate and as a result adults tended to respond to me positively. And I wasn't overawed by anything, which became a very useful trait when starting a band. Musicians need rock-solid confidence to express themselves and project their character through music. Pushing demos on record-label staff or asking for gigs needs self-belief. Just walking onstage requires a bit of chutzpah.

So while expressing myself wasn't really an issue, it wasn't entirely clear from some of my styling choices what I was trying to say! Though when it came to clothes I definitely wasn't the only one with issues. With his glasses and unruly barnet, Yog had been in need of an urgent makeover from the moment he first arrived at Bushey Meads Comprehensive. The two main offenders were his glasses, which he hated, and his hair, which he hated even more. It became an untameable mass of wiry frizz when wet, so rain was a particular hazard. Possibly easier to deal with were the specs. Yog became one of the first people I knew to swap his glasses for contact lenses, and being able to finally cast off the loathed 'bins' was a game-changer. His self-esteem seemed to have lifted considerably when he returned to the classroom in 1977. Contact lenses didn't seem to have affected some of his aesthetic choices, though. I

Me doing my Nick Heyward impression!

became convinced he was colour-blind when he arrived at school one morning wearing a brand-new coat.

'I really like the green colour,' he said, even though everybody around him could see it was definitely brown. The colour red seemed to cause him trouble too, but it wasn't until years later that Yog discovered he actually *was* colour-blind.

Despite all this, I never had to leap to Yog's defence at school, nor he to mine, certainly not in a way that was later described in the lyrics to 'Young Guns (Go For It!)' – 'Back off, he's a friend of mine!' He settled in well at Bushey Meads and got along with most people. As it went, Yog and I rarely took the mickey out of each other either. I knew how sensitive he was about his hair, glasses and physique, and so 'Yoghurt' was about as close to the wind as I ever sailed. When it came to our clothing, however, all bets were off.

The Bushey Meads Comprehensive disco took place a few times throughout the year. Held in the assembly hall, it was an event that in our imaginations had all the glamour of New York's Studio 54, or the Roxy in Covent Garden. It was also the only place where we could all get dressed up, which made it the essential thermome-ter of cool. But earning the respect of your peers was no longer the only reason to invest in some stylish clobber. The female form was now every bit as important to us as the FA Cup or *Star Wars*. We were approaching our fif-teenth birthdays and our libidos were in overdrive. The need to dress well was suddenly essential, especially as the school disco presented an opportunity for a slow dance at the evening's close. My success rate was underwhelming, but the odds never stopped me from trying.

There was one thing missing from these occasions, however – *Yog*. Despite my nagging he rarely joined us because he lived so far away. His dad often worked late shifts at the family restaurant and Jack, from what I was told, wasn't keen on providing a taxi service for his kids. So Yog missed out as his schoolmates boogied to the sounds of Chic, Donna Summer, the Jacksons and the Bee Gees beneath the school hall's threadbare light show – mainly a series of silent films projected onto one wall and some multicoloured bulbs to light up the DJ. And Yog was nowhere to be seen. I was determined to drag him into the party.

Over the coming months, disco was everywhere, helped by the release of the Oscar-winning movie *Saturday Night Fever* in December 1977. Starring John Travolta and featuring a soundtrack by the Bee Gees, its script was set within New York's club scene. Travolta's character brought the music to life as he strutted through the city streets. The soundtrack's lead single 'Stayin' Alive' had ignited the school disco the previous year and was all over the radio and *Top of the Pops*. Yog and I loved it. There was a taut energy about it that was absolutely irresistible. Then 'Night Fever' came out in February with a sensuality and slinkiness all of its own.

Empire Cinema, Watford.

Everyone in our class at school was talking about the film. It was a sensation, offering a glimpse of the world of sex, style and glamour that was unmissable. *Saturday Night Fever* lit a fire in us.

There was just one stumbling block. The film was X-rated, which meant we needed to be eighteen years old to buy a ticket. Given that in 1978 I was barely fifteen and Yog was several months younger, our attempt to fool the Empire box office staff was likely to fall embarrassingly short. We pressed ahead, hoping that by coming across as sufficiently urbane and worldly, we could hoodwink them. One way to achieve this, we thought, would be for each of us to rock up with a girl

64

on our arm. The promise of tickets, free popcorn and endless soft drinks somehow convinced two girls from our year to join us.

On the night of the film, I was nervous with excitement. I'd put together a clownish get-up of peach chinos, so tight that sitting down was tricky, a wide-collared shirt and black leather, metal-tipped, pointed shoes. I was perfectly on trend. As we approached the Empire, we decided that, given my confidence in the scheme's success, I should do the talking. Yog and our accomplices trailed behind, looking furtive. I stepped up to the ticket booth, pulled myself up to my full height and lowered my voice.

'Four tickets to *Saturday Night Fever*, please . . .' I said, pushing a five-pound note towards the cashier.

She stared back at me over the rim of her glasses, entirely wise to underage kids attempting to bluff their way into an X-rated flick. The crumpled fiver was eyed like a half-eaten sausage roll. *This isn't going to work. This isn't going to work!* An early bus ride home beckoned. I flashed a smile and she smiled back. Bingo! She pulled four tickets from the wheel and nodded towards the theatre doors. The four of us had bluffed our way in. *Playground notoriety was guaranteed!*

If our two companions had been nervous that some fumbling attempt at sexual exploration might take place in the back row, they needn't have worried. We weren't in the slightest bit interested. Once settled into our seats, Yog and I became completely absorbed. For weeks afterwards it was the focus of endless classroom debate. Back at Yog's house, he and I recorded a series of spoof radio sketches inspired by the movie. Twisted by our sexually inflamed teenage imaginations, a scene in which John Travolta's character Tony Manero pulls took on a life of its own. *Tony Manero gets a girl in the back of his car. He starts to fumble around under her dress only to discover that she is, in fact, a bloke!* It was all pretty puerile stuff, but it seemed hilarious at the time.

Musically, *Saturday Night Fever* was liberating. It legitimised dancing as an authentically male pursuit and provided a way to get close to women – in every sense. Until then, dancing was seen as faintly unbecoming of a red-blooded male. *Saturday Night Fever* changed all that. Being a bloke and getting on the dance floor was suddenly cool. Emboldened by our success at the Empire, Yog and I then talked our way past age restrictions and onto the floors of local nightclubs. Later, when our confidence was high and our parents' attention low, we visited basement dives in the West End, all of them hanging onto the coat-tails of Studio 54 and *Saturday Night Fever.* The summer of 1978 was beginning. Punk offered a rival outlet for teenage passions, but we were hooked on disco. For the next year there was nothing Johnny Rotten or Joe Strummer could say or snarl to alter our course.

All I needed was a girlfriend, so when my classmate

Jody invited me to her house party, several over-the-shoulder glances during Maths convinced me my luck was very much in. I fancied Jody, and Yog and I were looking forward to the party. He planned to crash at mine afterwards. On the night, I was certainly dressing for success: peach needlecords, which looked as if they were sprayed on, and a paper-thin, peach angora slash-neck sweater. The outfit was very much at the edge of acceptability for a suburban lad at that time. Quite what my parents thought as I left the house was a mystery. I doubt Mum was too fussed. My father was probably appalled. After arriving at Jody's place, I drank from a bottle of Bacardi, chatted with friends and mingled with dancing couples already tipsy on cider and rocket-fuel spirits. Suddenly, Yog grabbed at my arm. *There was something he had to tell me.*

'Andy, I don't know how to say this,' he said, looking a little sheepish. 'It's my mum and dad. They don't want you to come around to my house any more . . .'

I laughed. At first I thought he was joking. It hadn't taken a genius to realise I wasn't quite Lesley's cup of tea at first, but I'd grown to like Yog's mum, and she liked me. Unfortunately, she also knew I could be a distraction, mainly because my attitude towards education was very different to Yog's. He was keen: top O-level grades during the coming school year were within his grasp and his mum and dad felt that he could eventually make it to a fairly decent university, but only if he was able to stick on the straight and narrow. *No distractions, no negative influences.* That now seemed to include me.

'The thing is . . .' he continued. 'If you can't come to my house, then I don't think I should come to your house, either.'

I was completely side-swiped. *'What?'*

Yog's logic escaped me. But before I had the chance to argue, he walked away with a shrug, disappearing into a garden of dancing kids. I was stunned. One minute I was at a party having a great time, dancing and mucking around, the next I'd been banned from seeing my best friend. Yog had landed a psychological haymaker, one that looked set to break us apart – and just in time for the coming summer holidays, too. Already well oiled, and now distressed, I proceeded to get even drunker. I was soon slumped against the kitchen wall where I tearfully explained what had happened to another good friend and, more embarrassingly, Jody's mum. The evening became a traumatic blur. My last clear memory of the party was of being hoisted out of the middle of the street by Anthony Perkins's dad, who happened to be a policeman, until a hand took my arm and pulled me aside.

To my surprise, it was Yog.

'Come on, Andy,' he said sympathetically. 'Let's get you home.'

It was 3 a.m. The streets of Bushey were deserted,

but together we staggered to my house, Yog patiently shepherding me as we went. By the time we'd crept into the house it was daylight. I'd spent a lot of the journey home in the undergrowth pleading with the Good Lord for a swift and merciful death, but when I glanced in the hallway mirror I appeared to be relatively unscathed. The same couldn't be said for Yog. There was dirt and litter on his clothes, which hung from him like a patchwork of soiled tea towels. The smell he was giving off wasn't particularly nice, either.

'Bloody hell, that was a rough night, wasn't it?' I said, smiling.

Yog looked me up and down and laughed. 'Andy, how do you do it?'

I shrugged. 'What do you mean?'

'Well, look at us! I could make a dinner suit look like a tramp's pyjamas after one outing. *But you?* For the last two hours you've been rolling around in the bushes and there's not a hair out of place . . .'

He was right. I'd suffered an emotional bruising, though. But Yog's kindness on the way home had been a measure of his friendship: we were best friends, no matter what his parents thought, and it was going to be next to impossible for them to prise us apart. I was more convinced of that than ever.

And so was Yog.

5. Girls! Girls! Girls!

The summer of 1978 was set to become a formative chapter in all our lives. My classmates and I jumped into a world of disco singles, boozy parties and sexual exploration. Suddenly, it seemed as if we had become fixated by sex. Our mutual journey of discovery was set to begin. There was a tangible sexual frisson in the classroom and as the holidays approached, that young lust was given free rein.

There were always house parties during the long break from school. Most of the parents of our group seemed strangely comfortable with the idea that, while they were out, their home would become a venue. Permission was granted on the condition that the house wasn't trashed, and that nobody had to have their stomach pumped. After invites had gone out, a large mob would descend, expecting to drink, dance and, hopefully, get to know the opposite sex a whole lot better.

As well as the fumbles and one-night stands at parties, dating was fast becoming an emotional part of life

for everyone in our year at Bushey Meads. Well, everyone apart from Yog and me, that is. Try as I might, I
seemed unable to find a girlfriend. To me, classmates
like Katie, Lara, Anna and Charlotte were now every
bit as sexy as the girls from Pan's People. There was no
lack of choice. Eventually my luck began to turn on a
school trip to the Wye Valley when Charlotte encouraged me to slip a hand down her jumper. On another
occasion, Nina from 4A2 made it clear that she wanted
to me to go all the way with her. Given that I'd spent
hours just dreaming of copping a quick feel, Nina's
directness was completely overwhelming. I mumbled
some hopeless excuse and escaped, spending the rest
of the party feeling flushed and embarrassed.

On safer ground, however, my teenage libido was stoked by a stash of porn mags Yog found in the fields behind his house. The owner had collected a smorgasbord of top-shelf literature, including *Club International*, *Mayfair* and *Men Only* and stored it in a tin box. For weeks we sat, hidden amongst the wheat and barley, giving them our undivided attention. Next, we decided to try out a couple of the more mainstream adult movies. We kicked off with *The Stud* at the Odeon in Watford and then *Emmanuelle* at the Empire, a film about a Frenchwoman who travelled to Bangkok. It was what she did when she got there that we were interested in. And yet, while they were certainly a step up from the printed page, the X-rated movies were also a bit disappointing.

'These films are all a little on the tame side,' I said to Yog. 'I think we should try something a little more hardcore.'

He looked confused. 'What do you mean?'

'Well, Soho shows all sorts of dirty movies in the red-light district. Why don't we try to sneak into a cinema there?'

Needing little in the way of persuasion, he joined me for a trip into London. And to the Triple-X Cinema. It was everything you'd expect of a low-rent dive that specialised in blue movies: dingy and seedy and filled with men in raincoats fidgeting in their seats. I doubt it was the first time the chap in the ticket booth had encountered two nervous teens. The look on his leathery face suggested he'd seen just about everything before. It was clear that some of the other patrons were treating the film as an interactive experience. It was all rather unsettling and we left almost as quickly as we'd arrived.

But 1970s Soho had a whole lot more to tempt us, with suspicious-looking bookshops, alleys that glowed in neon, doorways offering the promise of dance shows, striptease and, in one, live sex shows. *Men and women doing it in the flesh, right in front of our eyes?* The very notion was fantastic. We approached the doorman, who directed us down to the underground bar. That we were both quite obviously not long out of short trousers didn't seem to bother him. We'd only just settled into our chairs when a hostess, in a corset and stockings, asked if we fancied a drink. Seeing as we earned our money from paper rounds and car washing, we declined the invitation.

'Sorry, darlin', it don't work like that,' she said. 'House rules. Every customer has to buy a drink. One each, plus a glass of champagne for the hostess, which is me, all for twenty quid. Now, what are you havin'?'

I coughed nervously. 'Er, I think there's been a mistake. We've come to the wrong place. Sorry for the confusion. We're going to leave . . .'

Instantly, there was a hand on my shoulder. The doorman loomed over us. His frame resembled a London telephone box.

'Lads, if you want to leave the club in the traditional manner, you'd better pay the nice lady first,' he said.

On balance it seemed a small price to pay. Relieved of our money, and without seeing the slightest glimpse of action, Yog and I left with our dignity in tatters, but everything else still mercifully intact.

By now, I was about to start sixth form with Yog, having passed my O-levels in English, Physics, Biology and Art, with a Maths CSE thrown in; I had decided to take A-levels in English, Geography and Sociology, but it hardly mattered as my interest lay elsewhere. Having decided the world of semi-legal vice was not for me, I refocused my efforts on girls closer to home than those of the Soho underworld. On the slimmest of evidence I thought there might now be some hope for me on the dating front. But for Yog, the process seemed thoroughly depressing. He hadn't helped himself with the brave decision to buy a pair of tight green trousers. He seemed to think they were the answer to his prayers. In fact, they were guaranteed to repel any right-thinking female. Eventually, he sobbed out his frustrations to me during a drunken walk home after a night out.

'I wore my new trousers and not one person has said they liked them,' he wailed. 'I must look ridiculous!'

There was soon better news for Yog on the romance front, though. Unbeknown to either of us, there was one person for whom his bewildering fashion choices held no fear. Lesley was an attractive girl with long, straight brown hair who'd been a classmate of ours since Yog's arrival at Bushey Meads. Now, in the lower sixth, she'd caught everyone's attention thanks to a rate of physical development exceeding that of her peers. She was good company and had a quick sense of humour. I'd fancied her for years and she had never shown the slightest bit of interest in me, but Lesley was so doe-eyed in Yog's company that he only had to crack the feeblest of jokes for her to laugh hysterically. And when our friend Tom held a house party, both Yog and Lesley seized their moment.

Tom lived a little way out of town and had put up a large tent in the garden for us all to crash out in. It would provide temporary accommodation for those of us unable to get home, while serving as a makeshift sanatorium for anyone who overdid it. Knowing I wouldn't have to check in with my parents until morning, I threw myself into the drinking and flirting with gusto.

It wasn't long before I found myself in the tent-turned-field hospital, a victim of some particularly nasty French vermouth. Trying to get comfortable, I wedged my head in a small gap between the ground sheet and canvas. When I glanced up I noticed a familiar figure wriggling against Tom's garage door. It was Yog! He was locked in an embrace with Lesley, his hands all over her. Fair dos, I thought, good going. I couldn't help feeling a little envious, but I had to doff my cap to my friend's success. My best mate had done the seemingly impossible.

Yog had got himself a girlfriend.

For all the fun to be had outside school, I was finding life in the sixth form increasingly dull. And I had come to the conclusion that there was only one thing that I wanted to do with my life: *I was going to form a band.*

There was nothing to lose. Life beyond school seemed fairly bleak, given the state of the country in 1979. Britain was in a mess, strikes dominated the headlines and the streets were filled with rubbish. Only the rats were having a good time. It didn't help that the growing dole queue was fast becoming a national crisis – everyone felt pessimistic about the future. Starting a band offered an escape route. And you didn't have to be top of the class in music to harbour ambitions of making it. As punk had demonstrated, everybody could play the guitar – you only needed three chords.

My horizons expanded as a result. Aged nine, the idea of captaining Concorde had appealed. By the time I'd reached sixteen, I only wanted to play music; to be in a band, to write songs, to make records and perform to the type of crowds I'd seen at Earls Court, Alexandra Palace and Knebworth. Bands like the Specials and the Jam reflected the national mood. At the same time I had lost faith in the disco scene, which seemed to be turning to soul music for inspiration.

When McFadden & Whitehead released 'Ain't No Stoppin' Us Now' in 1979, it felt like a disappointing turning point. Jeez, what's going on?, I thought and I began looking elsewhere for my fix. Punk had briefly excited me in 1977, but for its attitude more than the music. It was punk's successors that transformed the way I thought about music forever.

New wave had all of the energy of punk, but dropped its nasty aggressive edge, and bands like XTC, the Pretenders and Squeeze had found a far more melodic approach. There was real songwriting at work and it had all the tunefulness of the Beatles and Everly Brothers albums I'd listened to as a kid. When Elvis Costello's 'Pump It Up' exploded from my radio for the first time, it was as thrilling as Elvis Presley's 'Jailhouse Rock'. The radio blasted out exciting new bands every night and Yog and I were swept away by the likes of the Police, U2 and the B-52s. Elsewhere, the ska revival and a British reggae scene fronted by Steel Pulse and their *Handsworth Revolution* album were an equal inspiration. It was a rich and exciting chapter in the history of domestic contemporary music that would go on to inspire some of the biggest pop artists of the late twentieth century. Wham! was one of them.

There may have been others at Bushey Meads, such as Yog, who *liked* the idea of being in a band, but I don't recall anyone expressing it as a burning ambition, and while I didn't shout it from the rooftops, it had become my sole purpose in life. *I had to make music.* And there was absolutely no doubt in my mind that I was going to do it with Yog. We were so completely in tune with each other in the way that we viewed pop and rock – and life in general – that it was inconceivable he wouldn't join me, but I never had the sense that the ambition burned in him in the way it did me. At the time, I don't think Yog had any idea of the depth of his talent – and nor did I.

He also seemed reluctant to drop everything in order to pursue whatever musical aspirations he might have had. I'd first mentioned making music to Yog at the age of fourteen, then later attempted to talk him into starting a band when we were studying for our O-levels. But with exams looming, he'd decided it was more important to concentrate on studying.

'Next year, Andy,' he'd said. 'Let's get the term done first . . .'

I wasn't happy waiting, but a few more months of school hadn't put out the fire in me and I still desperately wanted to make music with Yog. While he was often interested by the *idea* of dropping everything to focus on making music – and I had been badgering him pretty non-stop – he was unwilling to go against his parents' wishes. Ultimately, it was a whole lot easier to say no to me than to Jack and Lesley and so, feeling the weight of his family's expectation, Yog worked tirelessly to get the right grades, promising me that once our A-levels were over, we could turn our attention to songwriting.

As I waited for Yog, other events were pushing me towards the formation of my first band. Mark Chivers, a friend from infants' school, had returned to Bushey after leaving boarding school. Over hot buttered crumpets at his stepfather's house, he introduced me to Joy Division. Their sound was a revelation and I was awestruck by their originality and the magnificent dread of Ian Curtis's vocals; the first song, 'Disorder', hooked me in with Bernard Sumner's pealing, ambient guitars. When I introduced Yog to Joy Division he loved them too, and they would become something of a touchstone for us because they were so markedly different from anything else we'd heard. *Unknown Pleasures* and their second album, *Closer*, became two of my all-time favourite LPs.

As well as turning me on to new sounds, Mark Chivers was also influential in other ways. Since returning to Bushey, he'd formed a poppy, post-punk band with some older friends in the area and they regularly rehearsed in his stepfather's house on Bushey Heath. Named the Quiffs, they thrashed through a series of guitar-propelled numbers. The songs were pretty good, but I was also drawn to their last-gang-in-town mentality. *The Quiffs were a crew.* The camaraderie they enjoyed when making music, writing down song titles or talking about the day when they might get to play a legendary punk venue like the 100 Club on Oxford Street, was inspirational. Sitting in on their rehearsals reinforced my own ambition.

Bands like the Quiffs often became the heartbeat of a social scene. They were cool to be around. The Three Crowns in Bushey High Street became the focus of social life with the Quiffs. On Friday evenings the room heaved with friends, many of us underage. I must have spent nearly as much stuffing 50p pieces in the jukebox as I ever did on beer. One night at the pub I learned that the Quiffs were experiencing an enduring problem: Mark had long struggled to find a perman-ent drummer and with an important gig looming, their latest incumbent had upped and left. If he couldn't find a replacement, he explained, the band was going to have to cancel.

I was struck with an idea. 'What about Yog?' I asked.

Mark listened to my enthusiastic appraisal of his talent, his timing, *his feel*. Eventually I convinced him, even though at that point, because of the noise restric-tions in the Panayiotou household, I had never *actually* seen Yog play the drums in anger! To my mind, the fact he had a kit in his bedroom was evidence enough that he was quite handy.

'All right, bring him along to the house for practice,' said Mark. 'What harm could it do?'

Quite a lot, as it turned out. The Quiffs unanimously gave Yog the thumbs-down after one rehearsal. Not because of any rhythmic shortcomings, but on his looks alone. He was most definitely not 'anti-establishment'. Nothing about Yog's appearance suggested he was cut from the same cloth as a member of Talking Heads or Siouxsie and the Banshees. By contrast, the Quiffs projected a cool 'art school' aesthetic. Despite Yog performing well at the audition, there was no way he was making the cut, simply because he didn't fit in. When Mark explained his reasons for Yog not making the band, it upset him terribly.

'Listen, don't worry about it,' I said, reassuring him during the walk home afterwards. 'They've made a big mistake – it's their loss.'

I believed it, too.

What I hadn't banked on was the extent of the fallout of the Quiffs' decision. Yog was already extremely sensitive about his looks, even for a self-conscious teenager. Though he had disguised his issues regarding his hair, weight and clothes fairly well at the time, Yog later admitted that the rejection had been a huge knock to his fragile self-esteem. I knew he was a little down about it at the time, but boys of that age are hardly blessed with deep reserves of emotional intelligence and I was no exception. I hadn't realised the depths of his anguish. Selfishly, I was also a little relieved at Yog's bruising rejection. The thought of losing my potential songwriting partner to another band was an issue I hadn't wanted to face. Whether having Yog would have saved the Quiffs from their collision course with obscurity we'll never know. Yog and I, though, were soon on a very different trajectory indeed.

6. Rude(Ish) Boys

Everything had changed. *I was going to form a band.* And Yog was joining me, whether he liked it or not. As far as I was concerned, nothing stood in our path. We were young, we shared the same ambition and I had enough enthusiasm to carry two people. And confidence, too. Following my piano lessons a few years earlier, I knew I'd be able to play the keyboards – at least up to a point – and Yog had his drum kit. Between us, we would find a way to write music. Yog maintained that music was going to have to wait until sixth form was over, but his words weren't entirely consistent with his actions. Despite his protestations that his studies came first, he'd been taking the train into London where he was busking in tube stations with our mutual friend, David Mortimer, who accompanied him on guitar.

When Yog and I bought tickets to see Genesis at Knebworth, David had asked, 'So what y'goin' for – the music, the birds or the ruck?' But despite his occasionally laddish manner, David was actually an amusing character with a quick wit and a genuine love of music. He was Yog's oldest friend, too, so I was prepared to cut him some slack.

While Yog's commitment to academia may have been wavering slightly, I was desperate for a change of scenery. I had zero intention of seeing out my further education at Bushey Meads Comprehensive. Sixth-form life had turned out not to be the hive of social activity I'd hoped for and I'd soon perfected the art of bunking off: I'd expertly fake my mum's signature by heavily tracing an old sick note with an empty ballpoint cartridge. I'd then follow the imprint left in the paper with a fountain pen to create a new and utterly believable forgery, which my tutors were unable to explain away. But after a few months of this the truth became inescapable. I hadn't done a stroke of work since returning to school in September. I'd had enough and so I approached my form tutor with the news.

'I'm leaving school,' I said, before classes began again after the mid-term break.

'Oh, that's good, Andrew,' she replied. 'Because we were going to ask you to leave anyway.' Clearly I wasn't going to be missed.

Yeah, I thought. But I got in there first, you old bag.

There wasn't time to dwell on it, though. If I was going to avoid a showdown with Mum and Dad, I needed my academic career to continue in some shape or form for a little while longer as I got a band together.

I phoned Cassio College, a collection of modern study blocks set in the old country estate of Cassiobury, and after blagging my way through an interview, I was accepted to take three A-levels in English, Sociology and Geography. Provided, that is, I was able to pass a three-month probation period. It was easy enough to agree, given that I had very little interest in actually getting any A-levels. My only focus now was to convince Yog to start a group with me.

With my place at Cassio secured, I phoned him at home.

'Yog,' I told him. 'We're forming a band.'

Despite his initial protestations, Yog knew he had very little choice in the matter. My confidence and determination were such that he had no chance. I was starting a band and he was joining it – no arguments. But while I was driving the decision, I knew I had a potentially willing accomplice. Eventually Yog relented, and once he'd decided to join up, he committed himself completely. I knew that he wanted to write and sing songs, and to develop his ability and love of music. I'd just nudged him over the line in what would become a defining moment in both our lives.

Everything fell into place shortly afterwards. David Mortimer, Yog's busking partner, joined the line-up alongside another guitarist, Andy Leaver, who lived down the road from me. My brother Paul, who had recently been given a drum kit for Christmas, was also brought in. We agreed that Yog and I would be bandleaders. We were the self-appointed frontmen and would share vocal duties, while, thanks to those all-important piano lessons, I also took care of the keyboards, although this was mainly brought to bear on songwriting rather than live performance.

From then on, I arranged much of the band's schedule, bringing everybody together and finding rehearsal spaces. At first this tended to be our parents' houses. Mum and Dad bravely allowed us to use the Ridgeley family home on the proviso that the responsibility was shared equally among all band members. But while the venue chosen for our first rehearsal was Yog's house, Andy Leaver's house became the preferred venue initially because his dad owned an electric organ, a keyboard being the one instrument missing from our line-up. Our parents helped us heave our limited gear in and out of various living rooms and church halls, and did so good-naturedly until we found more permanent facilities.

Our shared love of ska and reggae was evident in our songwriting. The 1979 film *Quadrophenia* had also provided us with some styling inspiration. The film, a story about mods and rockers on Brighton beach, had a great aesthetic. Everybody was sharply dressed in clean, pared-down suits in a look favoured by the Jam and a number of ska bands, not least the Specials. I hadn't known anything about the mod scene of the 1960s and its new incarnation offered sharp-tailored

A rare, early photograph of The Executive rehearsing.

A very early photo of a six-member version of The Executive, with George on the far right and me second from left.

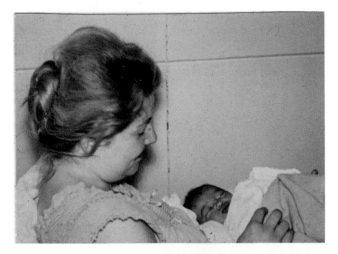

Left: A young Jennifer Ridgeley and an even younger Andrew John Ridgeley, 26 January 1963.

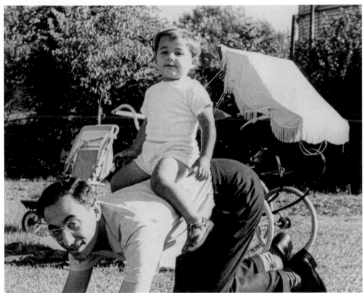

Right: Dad enjoying 'a quiet afternoon' in the garden of 23 Roundway.

Left: One of the very few photos of the whole family. Dad usually took the shots and therefore was hardly ever in them. This is a rare exception.

Above left and right: In Merry Hill Infant School uniform.

Above: An idyllic summer's day out on the Thames, 1970. A cherished memory.

Above left: Our home for many happy years: 40 Ashfield Avenue, Bushey.

Above right: Mum, Paul and I on a summer holiday in Swanage, 1967. A classic English holiday look: socks and sandals!

Above: Ashfield Primary School annual school photo, May 1972.

Above: Jumbo and Spitfire Willy in the back garden at 40 Ashfield Avenue, spring 1972.

Above: Summer holidays, and right, with Dad in Swanage, 1970.

Above: Mother and son with an uncomfortable looking Slinky Podge.

Above: The Executive. The definitive line-up.

Above: That jumper!

Above: Just the three of us. These were the very best of times.

Left: Eek! The shorts! The Club Fantastic tour, 1983. Those outfits! Our band has yet to forgive us.

Above: We love Shirlie!

Left: 'Andy, Andy, I've got it!' Chopsticks.

Above: ' . . . and would you supersize that for me?'

personality. He was a good singer, for sure, but there was little evidence of the range and technical ability that was to come. He had yet to mature as either a person or a vocalist. While he could mimic singers like Freddie Mercury or Elton John, he couldn't match them for power or assurance. Those artists had a conviction and charisma that Yog was yet to discover for himself, but even then he seemed at home behind the mic.

It might have helped that we were fronting the band together as the chemistry we'd had at school, and as friends, was immediately evident in those early sessions.

In rehearsals, we struck a nice vocal balance, even though this was the first time we'd ever sung together properly. We'd attempted it before, during those hours spent in Yog's bedroom, but this was the real deal and the pair of us immediately seemed to project a strong and energetic presence. We'd share choruses and swap verses. On some songs we would deliver the melody in unison from start to finish, on others we'd harmonise together. From the outset it felt good. I'd finally got Yog to commit to a band. We were making music together. I was rather pleased with myself.

We brought a tape recorder to our early sessions so we could capture the songs we'd been writing. A first track, called 'Rude Boy', took its influence from our favourite ska bands. Yog and I sang the words to a pulsing reggae backbeat:

RUDE BOY

MUSIC GEORGIOS PANAYIOTOU
WORDS ANDREW RIDGELEY &
GEORGIOS PANAYIOTOU

Rude Boy, Rude Boy,
" " " "
" " " "
" " " "

This ain't your party
No-one invited you.
You've come to trouble
Don't think we haven't noticed you.
You wanna stick around?
You better play it cool.
CHORUS
Rude Boy, Rude Boy
Naughty Rude Boy!
" " " "

You've been seen around
You've got a bad name
I've seen you skanking.
It look like you been named.
But you not one of us
You'd better play our game.

CHORUS

Break.

You don't take no heed,
Of what I tell you,
You need the strongarm act,
Aforced upon you,
Rude Boy!
You not so naughty now!   Rude Boy!
                                           Rude Boy!
CHORUS ....   Rude Boy!
                                           Rude Boy!
This ain't your party   ⌐   Rude Boy!
No-one invited you
You've come to trouble   Repeat to fade.
Don't think we haven't noticed you!

Repeat for three times

Rude boy, rude boy,
Naughty rude boy,
This ain't your party,
No one invited you.

In our heads it was a sure-fire hit and from then on we wrote quickly, writing at least one new song per session. 'The Executive' came next, its lyrics a comment on the drudgery of office life. We should be so lucky. Unless the band hit the big time we were more likely to hit the dole queue. But we liked the song's sharp-sounding title and the vaguely sophisticated image it conjured up.

We became The Executive.

At rehearsals, Yog and I wrote using whatever instruments we had on the day and we'd sketch out the melodies of the songs we were going to sing; the others would figure out the drums and guitar parts at the same time and gradually the song's form would take shape. Yog and I worked in much the same way as each other. My limited piano-playing experience aside, neither of us had been taught how to play any instruments and so we wrote instinctively. Yog was obviously very musical and picked up songs quickly through an ear for melody that let him express himself through music. None of us were competent musicians at that stage, but we both had enough raw talent to play the songs. Of course it helped that none of them were particularly complex or

93

difficult to play! Later in his career, George was rather disparaging about The Executive, but at the time he, like me, thought we were the bee's knees. And after a few months of playing together, I was more and more convinced of our potential.

Meanwhile, the same could not be said of my academic career. I was no more interested in my A-levels at college than I had been at school, but an environment that encouraged students to take responsibility for their own attendance suited me down to the ground. As a result, my social life was very much on the upswing.

Parties! Music! Girls!

Opportunity knocked at every turn and I travelled into London with college friends to see the American new wave band, the B-52s, whom I'd discovered through John Peel's radio show. That was then followed with an Orchestral Manoeuvres in the Dark gig. My horizons were expanding along with my friendship circle, but Yog was never out of the picture and the Executive remained our focus.

Encouragingly, when it came to the dating game, I'd also found my feet. Girls in the corridor were smiling – at *me*. While throughout my time at Bushey Meads, I'd drooled over half the girls in my class and barely got a sniff of action, I seemed to have been flung into an alternative universe at Cassio. And that's when I met my first proper girlfriend, Hannah. I had first noticed her during Geography when she'd sat down at the desk

in front of me. Hannah's crimped red hair caught my eye immediately. She was gorgeous and elegant, and when we talked after lessons, I learned of her keen creative streak: Hannah designed and made her own clothes, which only added to her allure.

Finally I overcame my nerves, asked her out on a date, and Hannah said yes. As two quite sensitive kids, we grew into our relationship slowly. Until, that is, we'd slept together in her parents' bed when they went away for a weekend. Then there was no looking back and when Mum and Dad announced they were going on holiday for a couple of weeks, Hannah agreed to stay

95

over one night. The next morning, as we slept in, the bedroom light suddenly clicked on. It was Mum and Dad! Home early, without warning. They hadn't quite caught us in the act, but they had seen enough to understand exactly what was going on. It was excruciating. Mum was livid and it took me a while to get back in her good books. Such is the way of teen romance that I broke up with Hannah a few weeks later after another girl at college caught my eye.

I'd turned seventeen and life was changing at an exhilarating pace. And that included music.

7. One Step Beyond

It's often assumed that where George led, I followed. That might have been the way of things by the time we came to recording *Make It Big* in 1984, but not throughout our formative days together. There might have been little doubt in his mind that music was where his destiny lay, but he didn't yet have the self-belief to bring it about. And while chart success for The Executive seemed a million miles away, his confidence in his own talent, as the band wrote more and more songs, was growing.

I had no such doubts about my own abilities. While in years to come Yog's gifts meant I was always going to struggle creatively in comparison, at the time, in terms of sheer, unwavering confidence, I was light years ahead. What was clear right from the very beginning, though, was that the two of us worked very well together and I was utterly convinced we would do something, *go somewhere*. My focus wasn't on fame, success or money, though. I longed for nothing more than a record label or manager having enough faith in us and our music to offer us a deal. The same dream was shared by millions of kids the world over. But not, it seemed, by Jack Panayiotou.

Even though I'd left Bushey Meads, Jack felt I was still distracting Yog from what he thought should be his son's true path. He wanted George's education to finish with a university degree, and on the rare occasions I saw him, I sensed he thought I was leading his son astray. But the relationship between father and son could be pretty fractious too, and Yog was fearful that pursuing his musical ambitions might strain it further. Hoping for his approval, Yog eventually summoned up the courage to play his dad a cassette of songs by The Executive. They were rudimentary recordings, but carried enough melody to suggest there was potential beyond the confines of a makeshift studio in a suburban living room. Yog pushed the tape into the car stereo.

'What's this?' asked Jack, suspiciously.

'It's our band, Dad. It's what we've been working on for the past few months.'

Jack was unimpressed. 'This is going nowhere!' he snorted. 'Come on, all seventeen-year-olds want to be pop stars, don't they?'

Yog snapped, 'No, all *twelve-year-olds* want to be pop stars!'

His frustration at Jack's lack of support was becoming palpable.

The 18th Bushey and Oxhey Scout Hut and the venue for The Executive's very first gig.

And some of our first solo band pics.

Not that it was affecting our progress. The Executive had arranged their first ever gig – a big moment for our band – at the 18th Bushey and Oxhey Scout Hut. Green paint flaked from the walls and a musty, damp odour clung to the furniture and curtains but to us it felt like Wembley.

We put up posters at school and college and word spread quickly. We pestered friends to join us, and took a more serious approach to rehearsals. Somehow the prospect of our first gig only increased the tetchiness within the band, though. If Paul's expansive approach to drumming was getting on my nerves, it was driving Yog up the wall. But despite early evidence of 'musical differences' inside The Executive, we stuck with it.

The set list for the show picked itself. We'd only written about a dozen songs and we augmented those with a couple of covers. We'd open with a rabble-rousing ska reworking of Beethoven's 'Für Elise', follow up with 'Rude Boy' and the rest of our homespun tracks, including our version of Andy Williams's 'I Can't Get Used To Losing You'.

We were all cash-strapped teenagers back then. None of us could afford the look we wanted: the distinctive rude boy get-up as worn by the ska scene's flag-bearers and defined by the label 2 Tone Records. Its logo was a mod dressed in a black suit, white shirt and black loafers. Everybody had seen the same clothes on *Top of the*

Pops and copied them accordingly, but we were stuck with looking like a mismatched teenage gang.

To ready myself, I'd visited the Sue Ryder charity shop for a stage outfit, this time picking up a bottle-green leather jacket, chequerboard scarf and a pair of billowing, baggy trousers. Our audience was in high spirits as we took to the stage, having warmed up at local pubs, and couldn't have cared less whether or not we looked like the real thing.

'Für Elise' got us started, but because of our excitement it was played at a far greater speed than usual. I bounced up and down behind my keyboard while Yog cut loose with dance moves inspired by Chas Smash from Madness. A hundred or so kids were packed into the hut and they seemed to pulsate ahead of us, as audiences had at gigs I'd seen with Yog in London. And after we'd exhausted our set list and been called back for a series of encores, I felt as if The Executive were on the verge of conquering the world. At least until we had to clear up afterwards and pack all the gear into our long-suffering parents' cars to be driven home. That hardly took the shine off things, though.

Our first gig had been a hit.

I was now more convinced than ever that recognition was just around the corner. Even better, following our first gig Yog was feeling exactly the same way – he'd loved it. And a tantalising glimpse of what might be was soon to follow. Through a friend of a friend, The Executive were introduced to an A & R man called Mike Burdett, a young bloke who had been taken on as a talent scout by a small music publishing company called Sparta Florida Music Group. Mike was keen to make a name for himself and came along to see us rehearse. He seemed impressed with our songs, but reckoned we were a bit rough around the edges. Nevertheless, he saw something in the relationship between me and Yog, and seemed to like the presence we shared onstage.

Mike certainly *seemed* keen and continued to drop in to rehearsals, fuelling a sense that The Executive were gathering serious momentum. Feeling that things were falling into place, we pooled our resources to book a studio near St Albans to record a demo. We each chipped in a tenner and even recruited a local saxophonist to add to the line-up for the session.

We decided to record 'Rude Boy' first. Yog and I gathered around the microphone in a proper studio for the first time. In a move we'd later echo on the intro to 'Club Tropicana', we recreated a party vibe at the end of the song by inviting our bandmates into the vocal booth to capture the sounds of a party. We recorded 'Für Elise' using the same spiky ska energy we'd played it with at our first gig, then topped it all off with our reworked version of 'I Can't Get Used To Losing You'.

To help the chances of landing a record deal, we organised our first photo shoot. Yog dressed in a crumpled

THE EXECUTIVE

Lyrics: Andy
Music: Tog

Boy you know it's been a bad day
So many things I've had to say
Each one said a total surprise
I could see the shock in their eyes

So now I'm out back on my own
A little wiser I have grown
It's the last time I'll walk this bend
Now I'll have time to make a friend

Outside I'm old inside I'm young
These past years have been no fun
As I lie upon my bed
My working life buzzes in my head

CHORUS?
I am the executive
Only got one year to live
Such is the price to pay
For the stress so they say

May I say sir? Yes you can!
I enjoyed being your yes man
Working with figures numbs your brain
Their clammy voices are such a pain

Every day around me so much tension
In the end I get sold all pension
Directors lunches line faster
Ten years on you get a free pacemaker.

Now with such extended life!
We, that's me and my wife
Going on a cruise spend all our money
I probably won't die won't that be funny

CHORUS
I am the executive
Only got one year to live
Such is the price to pay
For the stress so they say.

cream suit, which was overshadowed by a less than successful attempt at growing a Barry Gibb-style beard. Inexplicably, I wore my baggies, plus a style of hooped T-shirt I could have borrowed from Marcel Marceau. The photos probably didn't add to the chances of The Executive one day gracing the pages of *Sounds* or *Melody Maker*. Nor, as it turned out, did our demo. Mike's bosses at Sparta Florida were unimpressed with our efforts and chose not to take things any further. The news was a big let-down. Our hopes had been raised and then dashed. The disappointment was softened a little by a recognition that we were attempting to sprint before we could even crawl. It had been too good to be true, but our brush with the possibility of a record deal fuelled our determination and kept our hopes alive.

This was soon rewarded when our efforts to get ourselves on the bill at various live gigs paid off. We pulled off a real coup and managed to persuade the students' union at Harrow College of Higher Education to put us on as support for The Vibrators, a punk band who'd themselves once appeared on *Top of the Pops*. But while we were over the moon at the chance to play with a well-known band, we were concerned about how we'd go down with a room full of punks. Amazingly, after ten songs and an encore, we'd won them over and escaped without being gobbed at. More importantly, we'd caught the eye of a local journalist, who typed up our first review.

'There would have to be a very good reason for

not dancing to the music of The Executive,' he wrote. 'Even two broken legs may not be excuse enough.' We were later interviewed and I remember moaning about the fact we hadn't already been signed. 'We're still quite naïve about how the music industry works,' I said, explaining that we'd forked out around £30 in expenses to play the gig and the venue had only paid us in beer. In reality, I'd have happily paid the Harrow College students' union to put us on! Later, Mum proudly stuck the cutting into a scrapbook.

The fact it had named The Executive's two singers as Yog Ranos and Andrew Rodgeley didn't bother anyone in the slightest.

8. Melody Makers

Just as it looked as if things were finally on the up for The Executive, all fell into disarray. Our next gig was going to be at Cassio College – my home turf. This was an especially exciting prospect. All my friends would be there and it was a chance to prove that we were good. But The Executive were unravelling. Since our formation we'd brought in Jamie Gould to play bass and Lesley's brother, Tony, yet another guitar player. With three guitarists, something had to give. We made the difficult decision to tell Andy Leaver that we were pressing on without him. Then, on the eve of our Cassio gig, both Tony and Jamie left too! Determined not to cancel, the four of us who were left decided to go ahead. Despite never having done more than muck around in rehearsals, Yog managed to learn the bass parts to our entire set, all ten songs! Miraculously, he very nearly pulled it off completely. And after he did finally stumble over some of the bass lines, he simply improvised by singing the part into the mic instead. Helpfully, I'd provided the perfect distraction.

On the night of the gig I was wearing kohl eyeliner, while sporting another bold fashion choice.

The emerging New Romantic scene revelled in glamour and, influenced by the likes of David Bowie and T. Rex, sexual boundaries seemed to blur. Girls wore their hair short, men used make-up and every-body dressed flamboyantly. The look was set to a soundtrack of dreamy synths and pop melody. Gary Numan's Tubeway Army broke with their hit, 'Are "Friends" Electric?' and opened the door for a host of other bands, from Visage to Duran Duran.

My inner New Romantic found expression in a genuine Stewart kilt that had once belonged to my grandmother, the tartan offset by a pair of cream, knee-high socks cut with different-coloured tassels. When I first wore it to a party at Yog's house it only confirmed Jack and Lesley's suspicion that I was a bad influence on their son. To be fair, even Yog was confused. When he opened his front door he eyed me with horror.

'Er, Andy, is that a bloody kilt?'

'Yeah, what of it?' I said, opting to brazen it out. 'It looks cool.'

It really didn't, though. But it was more than enough to keep my friends' minds off Yog's bass playing at the Cassio gig. I strolled into the college common room with my head held high the next morning. We'd dodged a bullet.

With Andy, Jamie and Tony now out of the picture, our streamlined band returned to the studio to record. The Executive had evolved through rehearsals and shows and we hoped a new demo tape might force some of the labels that had knocked us back previously to realise what they'd been missing. 'Blood Is Thicker Than Water', 'Why?', 'Donna', 'New Adventures' and the snappily titled 'Tell Me Have We Met Somewhere Before' were committed to tape. Yog and Dave Mortimer shared bass; Yog and I sang; I played the guitar alongside Dave and everybody chipped in with backing vocals. The results were a big improvement on our first effort. The songs were better – and our own – and the playing had improved too. This time we thought we'd nailed it. There was no way the music industry could ignore us now. Yog and I decided we were going to hawk it round record companies in person. He now had a bit of free time on his hands. Although working harder than me, Yog had dropped A-level Music Theory and was now only studying English Literature and Art. As The Executive's designated representatives, the pair of us headed to London to secure a record deal. A keen student of rock history, I'd decided the only way to grab attention was to arrive in the foyer of a major label and demand that somebody important listen to our demo. 'You'll be making a grave mistake if you pass up the opportunity,' I told them. Everyone turned us down. We waited for hours and hours in a succession of foyers and meeting rooms, only to be told that we didn't have what it takes. The news was devastating.

Others are doing it better.

There's no hit.

It's just not good enough.

While Yog and I understood the odds were against us, we really thought that we'd cracked it this time. It was a bruising setback and one that was set to be compounded.

Following our demoralising failure to get signed, we pinned our hopes on playing live instead. Dave told us he was arranging another gig at Harrow College, this time as headliners, but he had become elusive and the details felt confused. Dates moved; it was impossible to nail him down on information. Frustrated, I asked Yog round to mine to discuss it. Tired of being given the runaround, we decided that Yog should call Dave and wring the truth out of him. In the middle of the call Yog turned to me and told me there was no gig. It had all been a complete lie.

I was furious. The gig had assumed much greater importance to us since the knockbacks with the demo and Dave had led us up the garden path. He'd lost interest in The Executive and we later discovered he had been flirting with another band. So Dave was out.

He didn't want us and we didn't want him. Then I gave my brother the news only for him to announce that he was leaving to join a three-piece jazz-funk outfit called Souls Valiant. Paul wanted to play in a set-up where he could give free rein to his more exuberant style. That style might have driven me and Yog nuts, but with Paul's departure The Executive were finished.

One evening he came home with a tape of his new band, but refused to play them to anyone but Mum and Dad. Unable to contain my curiosity, I sneaked a listen. In fairness, I was no great fan of jazz funk, but I couldn't help thinking, 'He left The Executive for *this*?' I resisted the temptation to tell him what I thought of it, but I suspect he knew. The damage was done though. Paul and Dave's lack of faith meant that Yog and I had been abandoned just at the point where The Executive had seemed primed for discovery. And so we only had each other. There was never any question that we would somehow carry on making music together. And we soon had a new sparring partner.

Cute, blonde and very pretty, Shirlie Holliman caught my eye in the Three Crowns. She had been in the year above me at school, but had left at sixteen and moved to Sussex where she trained to become a horse-riding instructor. She'd just returned to Bushey, and after I'd summoned up the courage to introduce myself, we hit it off immediately. She was warm and funny and I was chuffed when she said she'd go on a date with me.

Both keen, we agreed to meet up the following evening, which turned out not to have been the smartest decision. It was my eighteenth birthday. I enjoyed a few lunchtime pints with friends. I'm not sure what possessed me to choose Special Brew, but the result was that by the time evening rolled around I was unable to string a sentence together. Staggering home, I collapsed on the bed, my head spinning. But I still had to tell Shirlie. 'I'm so sorry,' I slurred over the phone, the room whirling around me like a ceiling fan. 'I've had a few birthday drinks and got a bit carried away . . .'

When we eventually met up again, I realised that tolerance, thoughtfulness and understanding came as standard with Shirlie. But she was also so much more worldly and independent than the other girls I'd met before. When I shared the unedifying details of a Sunday morning strip act at a Sheffield working man's club that her eldest brother had taken me to, she took it all in her stride, enthralled and repulsed in equal measure.

We were soon inseparable. I loved her determination to live life to the full and I told her about my failed attempt to conquer the record industry with The Executive and about how unsure Yog and I were about our next step. He had recently been invited to audition with a soul-funk group in North London. When I joined him for the session, I was relieved to find they were heavy on technique, but very light on songs. I was even more relieved when Yog was knocked back.

'You're not what we're looking for,' said the band's songwriter-in-chief, blissfully unaware of just what it was he was passing up.

On the way home, Yog and I decided that we would carry on working together. And I decided that it was time Yog met Shirlie. The three of us shared so many interests that I knew they would click instantly. When we went round to his house, she recognised him immediately.

'Oh my God, he's the geeky, specky one from school!' she whispered as we headed up to his room to rifle through his record collection. Happily she soon got over her surprise and fitted in right away.

In the weeks that followed, the three of us went club-bing together, preparing for nights out at venues like Bogart's in South Harrow by choreographing our own dance routines in Yog's bedroom. We danced to 'Planet Earth' by Duran Duran and Spandau Ballet's 'To Cut A Long Story Short' and 'Chant No. 1'. I developed a big swinging sidekick in the air that the three of us thought was brilliant, but must have looked ridiculous to eve-ryone watching. It was our suburban take on what we'd seen in London, at Le Beat Route and the Wag Club, rooms that were considered the epitome of cool by the New Romantic scene. We were young, uncom-plicated and happiest together. My grandmother even wondered out loud if there was a bizarre love triangle between us, but we were just really at ease with each other. So much so that Shirlie felt comfortable enough to tell me that she actually preferred dancing with Yog. 'It's like riding someone else's bike when I dance with you,' she said one night. 'You're too . . . *angular*.' And I didn't mind. Not much, anyway.

On Friday and Saturday nights in Bogart's there wasn't much room to dance in any case. It was always rammed and the weekend crowd tended to drink more, too. A big swinging sidekick was more likely to start a fight than bring to mind John Travolta. Tuesday was different, though: an 'alternative' night. The three of us danced to cooler cuts like 'Papa's Got A Brand New Pigbag' or Blue Rondo à la Turk's 'Me and Mr Sanchez'.

Your BRIGHT new Mirror
WHAM
goes to a party

WHAT a swell party it was. Wham's George Michael and dancing girl Shirley Holliman were clearly in close harmony. And their pop buddy Andrew Ridgeley joined in the fun, as you'll see if you turn to PAGE 3.
Picture: ALAN GRISBROOK

Sometimes Yog and I partnered each other; at other times Shirlie joined us in our well-rehearsed routines. But as we drank and danced, the friendship between us grew stronger and stronger.

9. Wham! Bam! (I Am! A Man!)

Britain was a tinderbox throughout 1981. I was acutely aware of the frustrations facing older friends as they'd left college and school. Students passed their exams with flying colours only to find themselves at the back of an ever-growing dole queue. Around 2.5 million people were out of work and in the inner cities tension had escalated into rioting. And while the fire and the fury in Brixton, Toxteth and Handsworth seemed light years away from us, culturally and socially, Yog and I saw the adult world as a harsh place to have to make your way in. So we lived in the moment. We were having fun in each other's company and the distractions of music kept us busy, which, thanks to affordable home-recording equipment, presented a possible escape from the boredom of a nine-to-five job, or, worse, unemployment. That was just as well, given that I couldn't have given a toss about school or exams.

As the summer loomed into view, the consequences of failing my A-levels became more real. My blasé attitude had stretched the patience of Cassio's principal, Mr Strachan, to breaking point and he'd put me on a second probationary period. I'd developed a canny knack for appearing in lectures just enough to give the impression I'd stuck to some semblance of a timetable, but my teachers' attempts to pin me down on any missing coursework proved fruitless. I was more interested in pubs, music and Shirlie than any attempt at pursuing further education. In the end, I decided not to sit my exams. There was really no point: I hadn't read any of the textbooks and hadn't written a single essay. I intended to wait for the results to be announced before breaking the bad news to my parents, which bought me a few months to think of an excuse.

We lived as if the responsibilities of real life were years away, though. David Mortimer, our one-time bandmate in the Executive, had landed a job as a swimming-pool attendant in Watford and we would hang out there. While a trip to the Watford Empire to see *Jaws* had left Yog terrified at the thought of getting into the sea, the pool held no such terrors. He joined me and Shirlie as we spent our afternoons larking about in the water. There was little chance of larking about at home these days. Mum was newly house-proud. We'd moved to Chiltern Avenue on the other side of the King George V Recreation Ground in Bushey and, with the upswing in our fortunes, Mum became far more precious about appearance and presentation. Our new house no longer had the same homely feel. With hindsight it was easy enough to understand. Mum had gone without for decades, all the while bringing up two boys who had wanted for nothing. I was proud of how far she and Dad had come. That didn't stop me getting annoyed that anyone under eighteen had to remove their shoes on entry. The impression you were entering a royal palace seemed a little over the top. And Mum and Dad were making me pay them £20 a week for the privilege of living there.

Yog was having a harder time of it in the Panayiotou household, though. Jack had issued an ultimatum:

'Get yourself a record contract within six months, get a job,' he said, 'or *get out of this house.*'

With that sharp kick up the backside, the clock was ticking.

As a result, Yog endured a string of mind-numbing jobs, starting with dishwasher at his dad's restaurant, the Angus Pride. A brief stint in the stockroom at British Home Stores followed, but he was eventually fired for not wearing the company shirt and tie. Then he sweated and grunted his way through a few well-paid weeks on a building site before he was hired as an usher at the Empire Cinema in Watford – the scene of our successful attempt to see *Saturday Night Fever.*

The two pillars of our friendship had always been music and comedy. A few years earlier we'd watched the Monty Python film, *The Holy Grail,* laughing so hard that I'd literally fallen into the aisle. Now Yog was able to bring me up to speed on the latest funnies as soon as they were released in the UK. He was also able to recite the scripts of all the blockbusters within days of them being shown on the big screen. In those days, films stayed at the cinema for weeks and weeks, especially if they were doing very well at the box office. Yog would have to work through the same movie twice a day, every day, for as long as a month. To relieve the boredom, he played a game in which he attempted to repeat a line of dialogue seconds before it was delivered onscreen. I don't know how he stuck it out. Having to watch the same film over and over would have driven me spare.

But Yog's work ethic was robust. He twinned his job at the Watford Empire with the position of resident DJ at the Bel Air restaurant near Northwood. While on paper this might have seemed like a dream ticket for a kid who loved music as much as Yog, in reality it was a pretty soul-sapping experience. The Bel Air was a chintzy dinner-and-dance establishment, in which the patrons ate three-course meals at tables positioned around the dance floor. During dinner, Yog spun records over the sound of clinking glasses and chatting couples. He was allowed to throw in a few gems from his own record collection, but he generally had to play more middle-of-the-road stuff. Too much ABBA or the Jacksons might have put people off their chicken Kievs.

'Good evening,' he would say at the point his set

interrupted the muzak. 'Welcome to the Bel Air, and now for some music . . .' But with his record decks situated behind a post, once he'd introduced himself, Yog just became another part of the bland restaurant furniture.

Despite his understandable grumbling, Yog was at least well paid, bringing in around seventy quid a week for his efforts. Meanwhile, I was not. I'd previously had a holiday job at Dad's firm, a camera equipment specialist called J. J. Silber, where I'd seen enough to know I wanted to give it a wide berth. I hadn't actually minded working in the warehouse too much. There was good banter between the staff and it was fairly easy to skive off. (I sometimes snoozed on a bed made from cardboard boxes, hidden in the maze of equipment and stock.) It only made me more determined to escape the prospect of a boring job in favour of writing songs and making music. After leaving Cassio, I passed up the chance to return to the world of camera equipment. But after deciding not to follow in Dad's footsteps, I became yet another of Maggie's unemployment statistics.

When Yog and I weren't working or signing on, we were dancing at our favourite nightclubs. At Bogart's, Capital Radio DJ Gary Crowley played the latest hits from the likes of Spandau Ballet and Talking Heads. Into that mix arrived hip-hop. Still a relatively new concept in 1981, it had emerged from New York's block party scene and crossed into the mainstream with singles from Grandmaster Flash and the Sugarhill Gang, with their classic 'Rapper's Delight'. Yog and I were both fans and whenever Gary played it, it was impossible to resist the lure of the dance floor – especially when Shirlie was around. She looked great in her tight black skirt and check shirt, her waist cinched with a heavy belt. As we twisted her backwards and forwards between us, a move worked out in Yog's bedroom, it looked as if we were fighting for her attentions. Then I grabbed her with one hand and punched the air with the other.

'Wham! *Bam!* I am the man!' I chanted to the beat of the track.

Yog joined in, repeating the words back at me. *Wham! Bam! I am the man!* At first, it was an off-the-cuff call; but it soon became so much more. 'Wham! Bam! I am a man!' captured the very spirit of our young band: good times, dancing with friends to great music, with a little attitude thrown in. It was a compelling mix and one that would set us apart and define us.

Given our youthful energy and enthusiasm, it was hardly surprising that Yog and I wrote a song together that was harder and *faster* than the music that inspired us. It fused rap's staccato spoken word with disco, just as the Sugarhill Gang had underpinned their own rhymes with the bass line from Chic's 'Good Times'.

Then we added pop, hoping that in doing so we might arrive at an interesting destination all of our own. The pair of us wanted to imbue our songs with snippets of our own teenage experience. We'd gone through the educational system only to face dead-end jobs, or the dole. At the same time, some people we knew lived off social security, but were happily blowing their limited income in dance clubs and charity shops where they'd buy vintage clothes suited to the New Romantic image. *But how to mix those ideas?* Unexpectedly, as we drafted lyrics together, the jokey chant I'd come up with in Bogart's became a lyrical springboard.

> Wham! Bam!
> I am! A man!
> Job or no job,
> You can't tell me that I'm not.
> Do! You!
> Enjoy what you do?
> If not, just stop!
> Don't stay there and rot!

The words were shot through with the realities of our late teens. Yog had tired of playing the same records over and over to a room full of indifferent diners, but in Le Beat Route he had witnessed the power of rap music and its ability to engage an audience. Another spoken-word-style, call-and-response lyric was added to the song we were now calling 'Wham Rap'.

123

Do you want to work?
No!
Are you gonna have fun?
Yeah!
Said one, two, three, rap,
C'mon, everybody,
Don't need this crap!

On its release, people made much of the fact the lyrics seemed to glorify life on the dole, but we were just taking a playful sideways glance at both our lives. Yog was the 'soul boy' in 'Wham Rap'; I was the 'dole boy'. Neither of us had any intention of settling for the drudgery of a nine-to-five job, while Jack's ultimatum to Yog provided us with a killer line too: 'Get yourself a job or get out of this house!' Propelled by the glamour of the New Romantic scene, hip-hop, disco and the frustration of life in 1980s Britain, we had discovered our songwriting groove.

Our gathering momentum couldn't have happened at a better time.

While I wasn't concerned by being on the dole, Yog's circumstances made him edgy. He had his dad counting down the clock and, around him, others were getting on with things. David Mortimer had left for Thailand, after somehow blagging himself a job there – but not before delivering a stinging critique of

his friend's songwriting ambitions. Yog waved him off at Victoria Station and as the train pulled away from the platform, David shouted out of the window: 'Yog, if your tracks were any good, you'd have a recording contract by now. Your music's shit!'

And yet, such was Yog's growing belief in his music that he couldn't have cared less what Dave thought at that time. He didn't even mention Dave's parting shot to me until years later. Yog's determination was as steely as mine; it was hardly going to be derailed by a snarky comment from a mate. And especially not now we'd begun work on another song. We knew we needed more than 'Wham Rap' to our names if we were going to score a record deal.

'Club Tropicana' was inspired by our own experience of clubs like Le Beat Route, Bogart's and the hedonism of London's New Romantic hangouts, like the Blitz. New Romanticism and the rebirth of the club scene in London had taken place a year or two previously at joints like Billy's, who ran regular 'Bowie Nights', Le Kilt and Club for Heroes. At that time dance-floor music had evolved from disco into different subgenres and the early eighties spawned a bewildering variety of bands that were blending the idea of dance and funk into an alternative sound that also drew inspiration from punk and new wave. Bands as diverse as Haircut 100, Spandau Ballet, Blue Rondo à la Turk, ABC, the Monochrome Set and Talking Heads ruled the DJ playlists.

Le Beat Route had become an occasional venue for Yog, Shirlie and me. Androgyny ruled the dance floor; boys and girls applied lashings of foundation, eyeshadow and eyeliner, their hair sculpted into gravity-defying shapes with large quantities of styling mousse and hairspray. The look was completed by silk scarves draped around necks, baggy trousers tucked into pirate and pixie boots. Some outfits looked as if they might have started life in the fashion workrooms of St Martin's. Others, like me, were bringing their imagination to bear on what they could find in charity shops. The outfits were both exhibitionist and eclectic, referencing everybody from David Bowie to Siouxsie Sioux. And we thought we looked amazing.

Le Beat Route was easier to get into than the Blitz had been – a club from which Mick Jagger had, famously, been turned away. Even so, it was still important to make an effort. Anybody judged by door staff as being *too suburban* was turned away and faced the walk of shame past a long queue that snaked down the street. There was no way Yog and I were going to risk such a crushing humiliation. I always made an extra effort, while Yog spent a small fortune on a scarlet suit bought from a tailor's on the then *über*-cool King's Road.

The New Romantics weren't the only tribe on display. Goths in ripped black jeans, bright lipstick and bird's-nest hair often turned up to lurk in the shadows. I shared their enthusiasm for Siouxsie and the Banshees and the Cure, but I wasn't so keen on the frequently spotted vampire look. Less aesthetic were rockabillies with their quiffed hair and the punks who still clung to the spirit of 1977. Yog, Shirlie and I felt right at home dancing within this kaleidoscopic gathering. With 'Club Tropicana' we tried to distil those feelings of escapism and belonging. I'd started to work on the song on my guitar as Yog and I drew on our clubbing experience – while still wanting to avoid some of the pretension and archness that could attach itself to the New Romantics.

We took the too-good-to-be true atmosphere of London's nightlife ('All that's missing is the sea . . . ') and spun it into a pop song, our words also bringing

On set for the 'Club Tropicana' shoot.

to mind the hedonism of a Club 18–30 holiday, pool-side cocktails, sun cream and lots of sex. This time we nodded to a new wave of New Romantic bands now flashing onto our radar – Spandau Ballet among others. Chic was still part of the mix, alongside a hint of Latin jazz rhythm. Disco too had renewed its claim on my affections. It was moving into interesting places again. The Gap Band's single, 'Burn Rubber On Me (Why You Wanna Hurt Me)' pulled me back in 1980 the moment I first heard it while listening to the radio in the bath. The synthesised bass lick was dirty; a heavy drum fill at the beginning launched a song that would become an all-time classic of funk and one of the definitive singles of my youth. It was at once raw and fresh. I was knocked out. This was the effect we wanted our music to have on people.

With the melody and driving funk rhythm of 'Club Tropicana' in place, Yog and I worked on the lyrics until they were around halfway finished. With 'Wham Rap' already done, our plan to showcase a clutch of tracks to record label A & Rs was slowly but surely coming together. And in the background, the component parts of another demo were taking shape. A tale of teenage heartbreak and dance-floor guilt, it was our unnamed band's first ballad. It would forever redefine the way the world viewed Georgios Panayiotou – the man set to become George Michael.

10. The Edge of Heaven

I was fortunate not to properly experience the corrosive effect of being on the dole. I didn't sign on for long enough to feel trapped or defined by unemployment. There was even a strange novelty in visiting the job centre. Well, for the first few times anyway. I knew I was only marking time until our new group was up and running. Luckily, Mum and Dad extended me some leeway at home, but like any parents, they were probably concerned about what the hell I was going to do with my life.

I had no concerns, though. I was going to move to London with Shirlie, who had got a job working in an outdoor-pursuits store in the West End. Her aunt lived in Peckham and was happy to rent her basement flat to us for next to nothing. It was a far cry from the thriving district it's become since. Much more *Only Fools and Horses* than artisan bakers and craft-beer shops. The flat we rented was down at heel and a bit depressing, so I tried to brighten it up with a lick of paint. It

helped a little but nothing could lift the misery of, in the absence of a bath, having to turn the oven on and open the door for warmth in order to wash in a freezing kitchen while standing in a bowl of hot water.

In contrast to this somewhat underwhelming experience of London life, my songwriting aspirations had been given a boost by a generous eighteenth-birthday present from Mum and Dad – a white Fender Telecaster with a black scratch plate and rosewood fretboard. It looked incredible and became a prized possession to rank alongside my record collection. Every night, I'd lovingly pack it away in a case, storing it under my bed because the room was so minute. In the evenings I'd

In my extremely small bedroom at 73 Chiltern Avenue.
It's unusually tidy!

practise over and over, piecing together covers of the songs I loved and trying out interesting chord sequences that Yog and I could work on together. One particular idea – which I'd come up with just before moving to Peckham – seemed to evoke a sadness, suggesting a plaintive melody and a slow-tempo rhythm. A few days later, Yog came round and I played it to him.

'What do you make of this?' I said, working through the chords.

He looked at me, a little surprised. 'Oh my God, Andy. That goes perfectly with an idea I've had going round and round in my head! Play it again . . .'

I carried on playing the chords, Yog singing what would later become the haunting saxophone melody on 'Careless Whisper'. Through an extraordinary coincidence, our separate ideas complemented each other perfectly. I don't know whether Yog had already imagined his melody working with quite the same tempo as mine, but it seemed to fit the song and so the two of us had laid the foundations. We slowly figured out the verses, choruses, lyrics and nuances over the next few months.

Sometimes we worked on 'Careless Whisper' at Yog's house in Radlett. On other occasions we wrote at the Peckham flat, although it was hardly the most creatively stimulating environment. Neither had the dingy basement done much for the romance between Shirlie and me. We both missed our friends in Bushey and she was fed up with her shop-assistant job, so it wasn't long before we returned home. 'Careless Whisper' came together. The largely minor chord-based progression I'd come up with suggested a lyric imbued with emotion and regret, and so Yog decided to draw on his own teenage experience. The tale he crafted of a cheating lover, hemmed in by guilt, was inspired by feelings prompted by two-timing his girlfriend, Helen Tye, a year previously. While Yog hadn't had any serious girlfriends since his summer romance with Lesley in 1978, he did have a thing going with Helen, a tall girl with exotic looks from his A-level Art class – her mum was Swedish and her dad was from South East Asia. Yog had even introduced her to his mum. And, given how much he idolised Lesley, that wasn't something to be taken lightly.

Trouble started when Yog was reunited with a girl he'd first met at the ice rink in Queensway when he was chaperoning his two sisters. While he waited around as Melanie and Yioda skated across the rink, Yog met a girl with long blonde hair called Jane. He fancied her straight away, but was still struggling with his looks and self-confidence and Jane hadn't given him a second look. Then, a year or so later, she turned up at one of The Executive's early gigs. Apparently she'd just moved to Bushey. Yog's thick glasses were gone and his hair was reasonably well managed and at first she didn't recognise him. But when she told him that she'd been impressed by his singing they started dating behind Helen's back. Eventually Yog confessed to Helen.

As we sat on the tatty sofa in that Peckham flat, his remorse was enough to help him craft the lyrics to 'Careless Whisper'. We both knew they were a bit clichéd:

> Time can never mend
> The careless whispers of a good friend.
> To the heart and mind ignorance is kind.

And we certainly weren't under any illusions that a poetic classic had been put together, but it didn't matter: 'Careless Whisper' yanked at the emotions; as perfectly suited to candlelit dinners as it was to dance-floor smooching.

Almost from the minute we first combined my chord progression with the saxophone melody that had first come to George on the bus to the Bel Air restaurant, we knew we had something special. Not everyone was convinced, however, and he later told people that his sisters ribbed him by referring to the song as 'Tuneless Whisper'. Both of us were absolutely convinced that the song had the makings of a hit, though, and George's growing confidence was now showing in his voice. As we wrote 'Careless Whisper' I heard the first hints of the emotional power that would go on to define his singing. Our new song provided him with the first real showcase for that.

*

We may have been making progress with the songwriting, but the band still didn't have a name. We needed something that captured the essence of what set us apart – our energy and our friendship – and then it came to us:

Wham!

There it was in our first completed song. The name now seems so blindingly obvious that I'm still not sure which one of us first thought to use it. Wham! was snappy, immediate, fun and boisterous too. Its comic-book-style exclamation mark also demanded attention. And yet both Yog and I were a little unsure at first. However, in the absence of anything else, we figured Wham! would have to do until we hit upon something better. When the word eventually stuck, we couldn't imagine using anything else.

With only three songs in varying stages of completion, we felt the time was right to make a first demo. Given our limited resources, the cost of hiring a recording studio was beyond us. Yog had asked his parents for a Fostex – a four-track porta-studio – as a birthday present, but was given a pair of antique guns instead. It was yet another example of how little belief Jack had in Yog's ability to make a career in music. It was a continuing source of frustration. George had done nothing to alleviate the intensifying friction between father and son. Luckily, we knew a friend of a friend who *did* own a Fostex and was prepared to hire it out to us for twenty

quid a day. We then recorded Wham!'s first demo at my house. My brother, now forgiven for his ill-advised journey into jazz funk, was called in to help out on backing vocals. We'd only had the money to hire the four-track, along with a Doctor Rhythm drum box, for a single day, and so time was against us. It was even more pressing for Yog. He was only too aware that this was his last throw of the dice; Jack's deadline loomed large. If our demo didn't work he'd soon have to make some tricky decisions about his next steps.

The pressure was on.

Given that it was the only song we'd written in full, the first track we recorded was 'Wham Rap', all of us chipping in with vocals during the chorus. I played the guitar, obviously Yog sang, and we all muddled along with the recording equipment and programming. Despite the fact that we'd not completed writing the two other songs, we pressed ahead anyway. We laid down around half of 'Club Tropicana' and even less of 'Careless Whisper'. Of all three songs, I knew that 'Careless Whisper' was the best of the bunch, and I wasn't the only one to have noticed it. When Yog later played some of the tape to Shirlie in the car, she loved it too. The next step was to tout our demo to any record companies that might listen.

Talk about confidence. We genuinely believed there was enough on tape for us to land a record deal. It seems baffling to me now, but back then we really thought we were that good. I think we were just emboldened by the new songs. We knew it was a huge leap forward and that in essence we'd written three hit records. These tracks were the cornerstone of Wham! and I was determined to make use of any lead and any available contact to try to get a foot in the door. I wasn't fussed about which label signed us, I just wanted a record contract.

I'd previously met an A & R man called Mark Dean when I was in search of a deal for The Executive. Mark worked for Phonogram and was always on the lookout for new bands. More importantly he was local, having studied at Cassio a few years prior to me. He'd shown some interest in the Quiffs and I'd sometimes chatted to him in the Three Crowns. But arranging to meet at his house with a tape of The Executive had still been pretty intimidating. My confidence wasn't entirely bulletproof and this was very much a business meeting. And Mark quickly dashed my hopes.

'Nah', he said after I'd played him 'Rude Boy' and the rest. 'This is a bit old hat. It's not totally without promise, but it's not for me.'

With 'Careless Whisper', 'Club Tropicana' and 'Wham Rap', however, Yog and I now had something more substantial to share. In the meantime, Mark's stock had risen sharply. By the end of 1981 he'd signed Soft Cell, the synth pop duo who were famous for their 1981 hit, 'Tainted Love'. Though Mark was now working at altitudes that seemed slightly out of reach for Wham!, I sent our new tape to him regardless, and targeted a list of other potential labels as we waited for his response – if there was one. Our efforts with The Executive had given us some experience of door-stepping record companies and Yog and I soon formulated a plan of attack. Both of us would approach the reception desk, claiming to have arrived for a very important appointment. When our fictional meeting wasn't found in the diary, we'd launch a pressurised appeal. I might sweet-talk the receptionist; Yog would become frustrated. We were quite the double act when we wanted to be.

'We've come all the way in, especially,' I'd say,

smiling winningly. 'Is there not some way we can still see them?'

'What do you mean, it's not there?' Yog would snap.

Mostly, our attempts failed horribly and we were turned away. By all accounts this was a technique that had worked for a number of bands during the 1960s. In the early 1980s, however, front-of-house staff working at record companies were increasingly wise to the game. On the rare occasions our ruse did work (and I'm sure we were given some time at EMI, only to be shown the door after the tape had played for fifteen seconds) Wham!'s demo was dismissed as not being up to scratch, incomplete or irrelevant. *You're wasting your time.* But neither of us were ever disheartened enough to quit and Yog became increasingly optimistic, having played the partially finished version of 'Careless Whisper' at the Bel Air restaurant. 'You're not going to believe this, Andy, people were dancing to it!' he said. 'The dance floor filled up with couples as soon as I put it on . . .' This was further proof our songs had serious potential – as if we'd needed it.

And then in February 1982, Mark Dean called.

'Andrew, can you two meet me in the Three Crowns tonight?' he said. 'I've got some news for you.'

It was happening. Mark was giving nothing away on the phone, but why else would an A & R man want to see the both of us? I told Yog to get to my house as soon as he could, explaining the situation without signalling my optimism. Though I was convinced Mark had heard enough to offer us a shot, I didn't want to raise Yog's expectations unnecessarily.

I needn't have worried. When we walked into the pub, Mark was already waiting, and gave us a fiver for drinks.

'I'm going to offer Wham! a deal with my new label, Innervision,' he said, delivering the words I'd longed to hear for years.

What?

'It's not going to be a huge thing,' he said. 'I'm taking a punt. I'd like you to have a crack at recording a single or two and we'll see what happens from there.'

Yog and I looked at each other, both trying to keep our feelings in check. Beyond clapping one another on the back, we attempted to play it cool. There were no whoops and no high fives. That just wasn't our style. But it felt fabulous to know that somebody else really saw something in us. I also felt vindicated. Our hard work and self-belief had paid off. Wham! was now in a position to produce music and I was about to make a record with my best mate.

Dad, on the other hand, was less than impressed. 'That's very nice, Andrew, but when are you going to get a proper job?' he said, barely looking up from his evening newspaper as I broke the news that night. As far as he was concerned, being in a band was fun, but

The shrine! 73 Chiltern Avenue.

ultimately a distraction. He certainly hadn't considered it to be a serious career choice with promotion opportunities and health-care benefits (plus a handsome pension plan). Thankfully, Mum got it. Only thirty-nine at the time, she understood the magnitude of what had happened at the Three Crowns, and hugged me tight.

Unsurprisingly enough, in Radlett, Jack was thinking along similar lines to my dad. He spoke with business contacts to check that Mark really was employed by a record company. He then hired a lawyer to make sure our contract was bona fide. It was a few weeks until we finally signed the paperwork.

In the meantime, Mark booked us into a studio to record a proper demo with session musicians at the

Halligan Band Centre in Holloway. On bass we had
Brad Lang, who'd played on ABC's debut album, *The
Lexicon Of Love*, along with a drummer who had previously worked with Dollar and Bucks Fizz. I played
rhythm guitar while Yog sang 'Wham Rap', 'Careless
Whisper' and two more songs, 'Soul Boy' and 'Golden
Soul' (which were never released because they weren't
very good). With those tracks completed, Yog then
pieced together 'Young Guns (Go For It!)'. Some of
the people we'd been hanging around with in the pub
suddenly seemed to be becoming very grown up. They
were moving in with their partners, getting married and
starting families. Once again, Yog brought a tongue-
in-cheek wit to bear on their changing circumstances.
And our determination not to succumb.

> See me, single and free,
> No tears, no fears, what I want to be.
> One, two, take a look at you,
> Death by matrimony!

Backed by another bouncing disco groove, it felt like
a dance-floor hit to match 'Wham Rap' and 'Club
Tropicana'.

As we worked through the recordings, our songs
were becoming fully formed for the first time. It was
such a far cry from the demos we produced in my
front room. Everything sounded fantastic. Played loud
through the speakers afterwards, the prospect of what

Wham! could be felt even bolder and brighter than we had imagined – *technicolour*.

On 24 March 1982 Yog and I finally put pen to paper. My mum excitedly made a note in what would become the first of many Wham! scrapbooks: 'Andrew and Yog signed recording contract with Innervision . . . WHAM!'

Our adventure had begun.

And almost immediately I managed to take a little of the shine off it.

11. Becoming George

It was entirely my fault that I'd split up with Shirlie. After we'd been together for a couple of years I took another girl to Bogart's behind her back. I'd assumed she was staying in that night and when she walked into the club with Yog, she didn't need to be a genius to work out what was going on. Understandably enough, she was angry and hurt and it took weeks before she would even talk to me again.

It definitely wasn't my finest hour. But we were very young. Having lived together, albeit briefly, we'd had one or two serious discussions about our future, but I wasn't ready for marriage or settling down. I liked having a girlfriend, of course, but was completely focused on getting a band off the ground with Yog, while Shirlie was working as a waitress in a restaurant in Watford and not yet part of our musical project. None of which really explains or justifies my infidelity, ·but there you are.

The way forward for Wham! was a good deal less

messy. By signing with Innervision on such a hastily cobbled-together demo, we'd sidestepped the pitfalls usually encountered by new bands. We never had to slog around pubs and bars, playing to rooms of disinterested drinkers in the hope of getting spotted. Yet we were under no illusion that the route to chart success was going to be smooth and free of disappointment. Yog and I were both up for the challenge, but it was made so much harder by our perilous finances. We were skint, and despite being set up as pop stars, both of us were still living with our parents. The £45 a week each we were getting paid by Innervision wasn't that much better than signing on. The difference, of course, was that we had a purpose.

As we prepared for what we hoped would be a string of TV performances and personal appearances, we took to rehearsing at Yog's house. When Jack and Lesley were at home we'd practise dance routines in his bedroom. But if ever they went out for an hour or two, we'd convert their living room into a makeshift dance studio to help us choreograph the moves for the songs.

To build momentum, Innervision had arranged for us to play a series of club gigs: small-scale performances in which we lip-synced the words and performed the routines for one or two songs while the DJ took a break from spinning hit records. Once relations between me and Shirlie had thawed, asking her to be one of our

backing dancers seemed like an obvious move. Given the bond we all shared, it would have been weirder had she *not* been involved. We recruited Mandy Washburn, a good-looking girl I knew from our social circle at the Three Crowns, alongside her. Mandy was only sixteen, but she moved well, was self-confident and good fun. To the demo of 'Wham Rap', Mandy learned the dance routines we'd worked on until the four of us were in sync. We were so keen to rehearse that on one occasion, after Yog had been asked to babysit for his neighbour, we all practised together in the living room while their kids slept upstairs.

While we prepared, Innervision's PR machine was moving into action and our debut single 'Wham Rap' was pressed at the factory. The label on the vinyl credited the songwriters as 'G. Panos/A. Ridgeley'.

Set in print on a record label, 'G. Panos' didn't exactly shout 'superstar' and that realisation prompted a swift decision. Like David Jones changing his name to David Bowie, or Farrokh Bulsara becoming Freddie Mercury, Yog understood the importance of getting the name right. Georgios Panayiotou was never going to cut it. If it was beyond his schoolteachers and friends, radio DJs and TV presenters didn't stand a chance. His pop career required something that was going to be a little easier to pronounce.

George Michael.

Although at first I thought making such a move seemed a little over the top, I had to admit that George Michael had a certain star quality. It had a Hollywood feel to it, like Kirk Douglas or John Wayne, and he'd settled on it easily. George was obviously just the anglicised version of Georgios, but he arrived at Michael because, amongst other reasons, he'd had a Greek friend at primary school with the same name. At the same time, George, as he was now introducing himself, was always keen to point out that he wasn't ashamed of his Greek heritage – far from it – it was simply that for a life in pop, he needed something that rolled, rather than gurgled, off the tongue. My own dad had pre-empted any possible need for a similar move on my part when he swapped Albert Zacharia for Albert Ridgeley.

George immediately seemed more comfortable going by the new name, but the change was actually much more than a mere cosmetic overhaul. *It helped to shape a new identity.* Over the years, he would explain how 'George Michael' became a persona, one that allowed him to navigate his way through a life in music and the limelight by helping him overcome the insecurities he'd experienced at school. I knew Yog had lacked confidence in his physical appearance, but, only nineteen myself, I was unaware of just how deep-seated the issues really were. As we readied ourselves for the release of Wham!'s first single, we were immersed in the excitement and anticipation of the job in hand and everything around us felt so positive that it just wasn't a subject of discussion. While it didn't seem to be hindering our progression during those early days as Wham!, beneath the surface George was still struggling with his looks, his weight and his self-image. The new character gave him a layer of psychological armour.

In his 1990 autobiography, *Bare*, George famously said that he'd 'created a man – in the image of a great friend – that the world could love if they chose to, someone who could realise my dreams and make me a star. I called him George Michael.' He never revealed who that friend was, to me or to anyone else; it's been speculated that he was referring to me. I honestly don't know, but it wouldn't have been a surprise because beyond me and Shirlie there weren't too many people that he

might have taken inspiration from. Others who were close to us also had an inkling of the dynamic within Wham! Our publisher, Dick Leahy, the one-time owner of GTO Records, always said that Wham! was George writing for me and a friend. The friend just happened to be George himself.

Maybe George felt that a version of my image and self-confidence was what he needed to make it big. Had he ever asked I'd have laughed and told him he was welcome to help himself to it! It didn't matter to me what he called himself and he was free to take his inspiration from anywhere he liked. If it worked for him, it was fine by me. I was in Wham! with George Michael, but I was best friends with Yog. And I wasn't going to deny him anything.

Before the release of 'Wham Rap', George, Shirlie, Mandy and I made our first public appearance, or PA, in Level One, a nightspot in Neasden. CBS, the major label behind Innervision, were convinced that a strong following could be built if we performed our songs on the club scene. They were determined for Wham! and their dancers to play as many shows as possible. The four of us piled into a minibus, and when we eventually arrived at Level One the venue was so big it resembled an aircraft hangar. The place was packed, and as the DJ introduced Wham! to the crowd, I noticed a major problem. There was no stage. We were performing in

the middle of a large crowd, many of them beery clubbers. As soon as the backing tape kicked in, Shirlie
and Mandy received some unwanted attention from
some of the blokes that had joined the circle of dancers around us. George and I tried to move around in
a way that protected them, but it wasn't easy. Our first
PA wasn't quite the party we'd hoped for.

This was the road we'd been set upon, though. For
the next few months Wham! travelled up and down the
motorways, playing gigs to people that either weren't
interested or were too drunk to notice. Regardless of
the people watching – and sometimes there were only
one or two – we gave every PA our best shot, convinced
it was the best way to propel us into the charts. We

acted like pros, but it was tough going. Sometimes we played three or four shows a night. Because the venues we were visiting were nightclubs, dressing-room facilities didn't arrive as standard and we often changed in toilets, or car parks.

Light relief was in short supply, but during a show at Stringfellows in London, I remember looking across to see George executing a particularly vigorous high kick, only for his shoe to fly off into the audience. It narrowly missed the face of somebody in the front row. Without missing a beat, George then kicked away the other, making his blunder part of the act; then he spent the rest of the show skidding across the glassy smooth dance floor in his socks. I don't think anyone was more relieved than him when the song came to an end.

Unsurprisingly, Innervision were incredibly tight with any expenses we incurred and looking after all the money was delegated to me. This became particularly uncomfortable when paying Shirlie and Mandy, whom the label had miraculously agreed to finance. I'd been given a wage book in which I had to scribble out their meagre earnings on duplicate carbon paper. It was the antithesis of what being in a pop band was supposed to be all about. It was also pretty awkward, reinforcing the fact that while the girls were an important part of our team, they weren't *in* Wham!, despite what people watching often assumed. But the four of us stuck with it and, as we drove through the night to our next PA,

George and I counted the bigger venues, like String-fellows, as small steps towards a bigger prize: making Wham! a chart success.

In the end, Mandy's heart wasn't really in it. She'd really wanted to focus on a career in the beauty industry, and when she then turned up late to a CBS meeting, George decided it was time for her to go. In her place arrived Diane Sealy, who was also known as D. C. Lee, and our shows became slicker than ever before. When we played the gay club Bolts in London, we were, much to our surprise, given live microphones. Then DJ Norman Scott spun the instrumental B-side to 'Wham Rap' and we had no choice but to sing it live. Happily, we pulled it off seamlessly, which only served to reinforce the fact that there was nothing quite like performing live. It had always been a big motivation for us, and was one of the main reasons I was so disappointed when the Executive broke apart.

We'd eventually have plenty of chances to play live, but first we had to embark on a promotional push for 'Wham Rap'. And Innervision were pitching us to the music press as something like the saviours of British youth:

Wham! A breath of fresh air Britain's youth are crying out for. Something rare, honest, young. Wham! are here to meet that demand. With all the vitality of London, but none of its recent pretension,

George Michael and Andrew Ridgeley will shape
the views, ambitions and pleasures of every adoles-
cent and make records that ARE teenage Britain.

This angle had a lot to do with 'Wham Rap's socially
aware lyrics, but neither of us had any desire to contribute to the political debate – that kind of thing was best
left to the likes of the Specials, or Billy Bragg. But we
were very keen to sell as many records as possible and
if Innervision felt that hyping us like this was the best
promotional tack, well, George and I were all for it.

And it worked. We soon received interview requests
from music magazines and newspapers, but when it
came to promoting our image as a young, vibrant
musical brotherhood, Innervision's meagre resources
were a challenge. We certainly had no stylist. The white
espadrilles that were a key part of the Wham! look cost
£9.99 and came from Dolcis. A few photo shoots in
and they were looking decidedly grubby. And George
had already lost one pair in Stringfellows. George's
favourite jeans only cost a tenner from Chelsea Girl
and they weren't even his. He had 'borrowed' them
from Shirlie and refused to give them back. We shared
just one printed, short-sleeved shirt between us. I
wore it during an interview with the *Melody Maker* and
George took it for a photo shoot and interview with
The Face, leaving me to wear a string vest that George
had worn during a record company photo shoot in

Corfu. Beyond that, I only had about three shirts and one pair of trousers!

Even with our limited sartorial resources, the reaction to 'Wham Rap' was positive. *Sounds* described us as 'socially aware funk'. The *Watford Observer* told its readers 'Wham! are a band to watch out for.' And then, despite glowing reviews, 'Wham Rap' barely made the top 100, getting no further than number 91. It was a bitter disappointment. Concerned, our publishers called around various record shops asking why such a well-received single had performed so underwhelmingly. It quickly transpired that 'Wham Rap' hadn't been widely distributed. Anyone wanting to buy a copy would have been hard pushed to find one. This revelation sparked something of a reaction in George. While he had an artist's sensibility, he also had a hard-nosed business acumen about him; in that respect, at least, he was cut from the same cloth as his father. Following the failure of our debut, he became obsessed with the distribution, regional sales and chart data for every Wham! release from then on. He was that desperate to build on our brand. It also hadn't helped that the single was embroiled in something of a controversy. Some critics claimed we'd glorified life on the dole, which wasn't the case at all, but we sensed it might have contributed to our modest radio play. We at least had a fan in Radio 1's legendary John Peel, but given his show aired close to midnight, he was unlikely to be hitting our target audience.

Annoyingly, the money Innervision *did* spend often missed the mark. Prior to the release of 'Wham Rap', George and I were sent to New York to remix the single with studio producer François Kevorkian. He was famous for working with the US duo D-Train, the band responsible for the 1981 hit 'You're The One For Me', and both of us were thrilled. New York was a city we'd dreamt of visiting ever since watching *Saturday Night Fever*, but the whole trip proved troublesome from the get-go. Innervision failed to secure our work visas in time so we were forced to visit the US Embassy on the day of the flight. After a breakneck drive to Heathrow, we arrived with minutes to spare. Ordinarily this wouldn't have presented too many problems, but I'd fractured a metatarsal during a game of football in Regent's Park. I was in agony, running for a plane was impossible, and as I hopped and grimaced through the airport, the crutches burning my armpits, it didn't go down well with George.

'Bloody hell, Andrew!' he yelled. 'Can't you go any faster?'

I flashed him a look. 'I didn't do this on purpose, you know . . .'

This type of exchange wasn't unusual for me and George. Neither of us was very keen on conceding points and contentious issues were usually picked over at length. Nor would either of us let the other have the final word *too* easily and so we sniped over the small things. We lived in each other's pockets and knew each other so well that most of the time we felt like brothers. So we bickered like brothers too. There were never any irreconcilable fallings-out, though, musical or otherwise. We wouldn't let them escalate. It was just as well because as we reached the departure gates, they were already pulling the jetway in. We begged the airline staff to let us on, but to no avail.

When we finally landed in the Big Apple, twenty-four hours late, we went straight to the Mayflower Hotel on Central Park West – an old 1920s building that was understated but comfortable enough. Or would have been, if Innervision hadn't booked us into a double room instead of a twin, which meant we had to stuff pillows down the middle of the bed to ensure respectable sleeping arrangements. For some reason the thought that George and I were going to share bothered the hotel staff. Successfully persuading them it would be OK didn't mark the end of our troubles. Halfway through the trip two burly security guards knocked on our door in the middle of the night.

'Gentlemen, we've checked the records and your bill hasn't been paid,' said one.

I was confused. 'What do you mean it hasn't been paid? Our record label have sorted the payments.'

Both men shook their heads. We had to leave. Despite Mark Dean's assurances that everything 'had been taken care of', it evidently hadn't. A frantic call to

CBS in New York later that morning eventually saved us from an ignominious eviction. And thankfully, we weren't in the hotel enough to care.

After *Saturday Night Fever,* experiencing the city's best clubs was our priority and we were curious to discover the beating heart of Manhattan's dance scene. Surprisingly, the more cutting-edge venues were no more than vast spaces, old warehouses or commercial buildings. Most of them were stark and uncomfortable, but *everywhere* was uncomfortable for me given I was moving around on crutches. To make matters worse, jet lag had worn me down and I spent one night sleeping next to a gigantic speaker as George befriended a group of young New Yorkers. When I woke up, I found they were considering going on somewhere else and he wanted to go with them. I was a little worried at first. We were at the arse end of town and New York had a reputation for being a pretty sketchy city at that time. But George had seen good times ahead and wasn't going to think twice about my concerns.

Fortunately the night eventually played out without incident. It's more than can be said for François Kevorkian's remix. When it was sent to us after our return to London, it was nothing like we'd hoped.

Both of us hated it.

If our first trip to America had taught Wham! anything, it was that the life of a pop star could be very curious indeed.

12. Party Nights and Neon Lights

And then *Top of the Pops* happened.

We appeared on the Beeb's flagship music show as a result of a freakish turn of events. Not that we cared how it happened – we were so eager back then. 'Young Guns (Go For It!)' had been released in September 1982, but with it only landing at number 73 in the charts, the odds of Wham! becoming internationally famous were lengthening by the day. While neither of us expected a top-twenty chart entry, this was a big disappointment and everyone from our radio-plugger to Mark Dean was feeling jittery. However, when the charts came out the following week, 'Young Guns' had jumped to number 48 and all of a sudden the prospects of a Top 40 record and of being included on the all-important radio playlists was within reach. Then the bottom seemed to drop out of our world. In week three of its release, the single dropped to number 52. Despite all the PAs we'd done and the acres of print that heralded us as ones to watch, it seemed like failure was staring us in the face. It was calamitous and George took it badly. I was also seriously worried, but I simply couldn't believe that this was going to be the end of it.

'Come on, it's not that bad,' I said as our second release slumped down the charts. 'We've got this far. It's only a bump in the road.' But George's mood was bleak. And with good reason. There was nothing more we could do to change its fortunes. I knew it and he knew it. Years later he claimed to have been almost suicidal at the news of the single's stagnation. The sense that it might be all over before it had even begun was sickening.

And then, in a heartbeat, our luck changed. Wham! was spotted by the children's TV show *Saturday Superstore*. We'd been performing to yet another room full of apparently uninterested, boozy clubbers in London when one of the crowd was struck by the novelty and energy of our 'Young Guns' routine. And she happened to be one of the show's researchers. We were invited to appear the following weekend. It was an amazingly lucky break! The programme was a big deal at the time and always featured bands it knew would appeal to its young audience. Everybody knew that an exciting performance in the studio could work wonders for a new act. After watching the *Superstore* in the morning, viewers then tended to spend their pocket money on records in the afternoon. It was a heaven-sent lifeline and we jumped at the chance to appear.

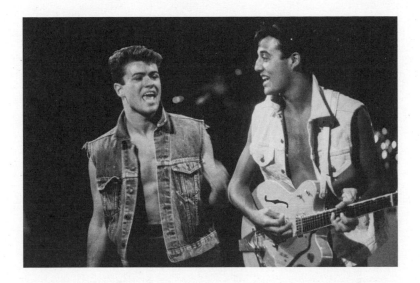

We knew it had the potential to generate the momentum we so badly needed. And we put on a real show. Backed by a band and flanked by a pair of American muscle cars, we played 'Wham Rap' and 'Young Guns'. Our performance generated an immediate upswing in fortunes. 'Young Guns' moved up the charts, but only as far as number 42. It hadn't broken us into the all-important Top 40. While it was a huge step in the right direction, we were still in limbo. 'We're only going to get onto the radio chart shows if we can somehow sneak into the Top 40,' said George in frustration. '*Top of the Pops* definitely won't put us on if we're only at 42.'

There was no getting round it.

While there were other TV shows like *The Old Grey*

Whistle Test that did look beyond the Top 40, they only really focused on rock bands, or folk and country artists. For a while, it looked like our appearance on *Saturday Superstore* might represent the dizziest heights of our success. And if both Wham! singles sank without trace there was every chance Mark Dean would drop us. Having got this far it was inconceivable that this could be the end of the road.

What happened next was the single most important event in Wham!'s success. Unexpectedly, miraculously, *Top of the Pops* decided they wanted to have us on the show. There's still something of a mystery surrounding the circumstances of our appearance, but apparently another band had dropped out at the very last minute.

166

I don't know who it was and we were never told, but fate stepped in and gifted us our golden opportunity. Anxious for a replacement act, one that could turn up at short notice, the producers scrutinised the weekly charts. Wham! came to their attention for two reasons. The first was that we were moving up the charts and had jumped to a position just outside the Top 40. The second was that we were a UK band, and able to drop everything at short notice. They called Innervision to ask if we could do it. *There was only one answer to that.* We grabbed the chance with both hands.

If somebody had told me when I was twelve that one day I'd be appearing on *Top of the Pops*, I'd have thought they were completely nuts. Both Yog and I had been such great fans of *TOTP* for so long, and following in the footsteps of some of our favourite bands gave us a huge rush of excitement. Neither of us slept very well on the eve of the recording. And while this was partly due to nerves, Innervision's customary attention to detail didn't help. The night before Wham!'s big break, we'd been booked into a King's Cross hotel that probably rented beds out by the hour. And George looked to have been given the worst room in the dump.

'What the bloody hell's that?' he said, pointing to the child's bed in his room as we arrived. 'Is that really for me?'

The bedlinen was made from some sort of nylon, and underneath, a plastic sheet protected the stained mattress from further soiling. My bedclothes were no better, but at least my bed was the right size. With his feet dangling off the end of the mattress, George had a terrible night's sleep. A room cost £10 a night and even that was a rip-off. By the time we'd arrived at the BBC studios for our start time of 7.30 a.m., both of us were tired, irritable and wondering why we had to be there twelve hours before the show went out.

That wasn't the only hitch. In a sign of things to come, George's hair became the main focus and he spent hours in the BBC's make-up department. His curls were blow-dried, straightened, hairsprayed and teased until he was happy with its appearance. To everyone else it looked exactly the same as it had done before the whole rigmarole got under way. Sensing that any hair-related ribbing might precipitate a complete sense-of-humour failure, I left George to it, resisting any temptation to poke fun.

TV studios, I quickly learned, could be frustrating places. The *Top of the Pops* experience flitted between being stressful and incredibly dull. We were both a little nervous and this wasn't helped by the high-handed way that the show was run. There was no doubt where the power lay in the relationship between *TOTP* and a new act like us. We were patronised and ordered around all day. It was impossible not to get the feeling that we were regarded as a flash-in-the-pan act and not really worth treating with respect. We were forced to repeat our routines over and over and over. We'd been on the road for weeks and our dance routines were incredibly tight, and so the fuss seemed ridiculous. It was all a far cry from the welcome we'd enjoyed on *Saturday Superstore*.

But it was worth it.

When later that evening we came to record our performance, a nervous energy crackled about the place. I'd become more and more comfortable when playing in clubs, but this was the big time. I looked across at George as we waited backstage. This was our chance, the opportunity we'd dreamt of, even as far back as our days as the Executive. With the Radio 1 DJ Mike Smith set to introduce us, our backing band packed together onto a small stage. George and I took our places in the middle with Shirlie and Dee, a studio audience waiting around us. There was a bank of cameras, lights and studio hands clutching clipboards ahead. I gave George a nod. *Let's do this.* And then the music started in a swell of funk grooves and stabbing trumpets.

> Hey sucker!
> (What the hell's got into you?)

George's rap kicked in. I danced behind Shirlie while she twirled and strutted in a fitted white dress.

> Hey sucker!
> (Now there's nothing that you can do.)

On the other side, Dee wagged her finger at Shirlie, a part of our well-rehearsed routine. But it was George who stole the camera's focus.

> Well I hadn't seen your face around town awhile,
> So I greeted you with a knowing smile.
> When I saw that girl upon your arm,
> I knew she'd won your heart with a fatal charm.

George was bare-chested beneath a brown leather waistcoat, looking fit and lean, toned by months of club PAs. Every inch the ready-made pop star. The image was as eye-catching as his performance was electric.

> See me, single and free.
> No tears, no fears, what I want to be.

Wham! had arrived.

As the music faded away and the applause and screams rang out, George looked across at me and beamed.

'Andrew, this is it,' he said as we walked backstage together. 'This is what I want to do for the rest of my life.'

I nodded, and the thought occurred to me: 'And now there's nothing to stop us . . .'

I was right. My faith in Wham! was justified. Before long, 'Young Guns' was a number 3 hit in the UK charts and we were the latest pop name on everybody's lips. Our band was about to rule the airwaves and Innervision were making plans for a follow-up single and a

studio album. The world we'd known was about to turn upside down. When I got home and walked through the front door that evening, Mum was there to crack open a bottle of champagne in celebration. The cork rocketed into the ceiling with a loud bang and dented a polystyrene tile.

It would serve as a permanent reminder of the night when the nation first took Wham! to its heart.

PART TWO
Making It Big!

13. Freedom

'Young Guns (Go For It!)' lit the touch paper and the hits kept coming. 'Wham Rap' was rereleased in January 1983, where it surged to number 8 in the UK charts, helped by the momentum generated by our first *Top of the Pops* appearance (and the fact that it was a bloody great pop song!). It was helped on its way by a promo video that depicted us living the lyrics: George strutting moodily down the street in a leather jacket and white T-shirt; me slumped in a chair at my fictional parents' house. God knows what Jack Panos must have thought as two actors playing my mum and dad yelled the line he'd inspired his son to write: 'Get yourself a job!' The follow-up, 'Bad Boys', hit number 2 in the charts and landed us another spot on *Top of the Pops* as Wham! began to become a household name.

But George was uncomfortable. Under pressure to deliver a repeat hit, he'd written 'Bad Boys' to the same formula as 'Wham Rap' and 'Young Guns', returning to the themes of teenage frustration and parental disappointment.

> Dear Mummy, dear Daddy,
> Now I'm nineteen as you see,
> I'm handsome, tall, and strong.
> So what the hell gives you the right to look at me
> As if to say, 'Hell, what went wrong?'

'Bad Boys' was undoubtedly slicker and more sophisticated than 'Wham Rap' and I thought it was a great single. But George felt its lyrical ideas had been overegged. Even the rugged look of denim and leather we'd adopted for the video annoyed him. And this time I wholeheartedly agreed. The styling didn't suit the exuberant attitude we were trying to deliver and instead reinforced the 'social warriors' label that some in the music press had attached to us. We'd been all for it when Innervision's press team had gone down this route, but we were learning fast. We had to take ownership of our image and music. And George, having decided he'd written 'Bad Boys' to order, distanced himself from the song's success. Despite the public's affection for it, it was only reluctantly included on Wham!'s greatest hits compilation *The Final*, but was omitted from the 1997 release *The Best of Wham!: If You Were There*. At the time, though, it still meant we now had almost half the debut album we were calling *Fantastic*.

A fourth song, 'Club Tropicana', had been upgraded from its early demos and was worked up in Maison

Rouge Studios in London – as was the rest of *Fantastic* – by producer Steve Brown. Like much of our early material, 'Club Tropicana' was a joint effort. The rhythmic bass line played by Deon Estus had a Latin feel to it, and he and I created the grooves that opened the song. As 'Club Tropicana' gathered more layers, I wanted to amplify the mood of sun, sex and sangria. 'What if we started the track with some sound effects?' I said as we recorded, imagining the noise of a car pulling into the driveway of a luxurious hotel, the click-clack of high heels making their way towards a party, and a pulsing bass and guitar lick that grew louder with every step. After visiting a sound library, I gathered together samples of a party in full flow, some stilettos walking along a pavement and the growl of an MGB GT sports car coming to a stop. The song's distinctive intro set the tone for the musical good times that followed.

As the album was recorded, George became increasingly at home in the studio. Though Steve, who'd previously worked with Elton John, was charged with the producer's role, George did a lot of work himself. He was directing the process throughout, and it was clear, even then, that he knew how to make a hit album. We both did. We'd spent our formative years together, developing a musical sensibility that often saw us share the same instincts for what we wanted. And there was a strong sense of how we wanted our debut to sound. Of course, the final arrangements differed in detail from the ideas in our heads, but that was because we now had access to things like live brass sections or sound effects. But throughout the making of *Fantastic*, George was in charge. He relished being at the helm and it later came as no surprise that he went on to be a capable producer on his own records. He was able to command the entire studio-recording process while I was happy just being part of it.

With our debut album nearing completion, Innervision became increasingly excited about Wham!'s potential, but George and I began to resent the way we'd been treated. Even though we'd now had three hit singles, we were still being paid a measly allowance. With our burgeoning success it felt as if we should be enjoying greater financial reward, but Innervision were having none of it. We were stuck with the original deal. And that turned out, once we were better informed about it, to be a very poor deal indeed. It became a source of considerable friction between us and Mark Dean. With the album nearly done, George's frustration with Innervision's refusal to revisit the contract came to a head when he decided to withhold the master tapes. His plan was to take them from the studio and bury them in his back garden. In the end, our publisher, Dick Leahy, talked him out of taking such a nuclear option.

'Get a hit record first, George,' said Dick. 'Then you'll be in a better position to renegotiate a good deal for yourself.'

With Simon Napier-Bell.

It was clear that Wham! needed some form of management to try to sort it out and make sure we steered clear of any further business pitfalls. It came in the form of Jazz Summers, a former army musician turned manager, and the pop impresario Simon Napier-Bell – a figure famous for previously managing the Yardbirds, Marc Bolan and Ultravox, as well as co-writing Dusty Springfield's first number 1 single, 'You Don't Have To Say You Love Me'. Together they called themselves Nomis – Simon backwards. George and I met them at Simon's elegant London home in Bryanston Square, which he shared with his two boyfriends, around the time of *Fantastic*'s completion. I liked Simon, he was a charismatic character whose attitude to life wasn't half full, but *overflowing*. He was engaging, ebullient and quick-witted. And *very* good company, as every good music manager should be. There was also an appealingly mischievous and anti-establishment edge to Simon. He chimed with Wham!'s unique image.

Jazz was the perfect foil. While Simon was full of big ideas and grand plans, Jazz dealt with the fine details and minutiae required to actually execute them. He was the bridge between concept and reality. I liked him a lot too, but I had a stronger connection with Simon. Mum and Dad had never put limits or constraints around me and my brother and so, like Simon, I was always inclined to follow a dream or take a leap of faith.

George's stricter upbringing, and the expectations of his parents when he was a school kid, perhaps made him more cautious. That might have been why he was more unsure of Jazz and Simon's management style during our first meeting or two. But he was getting to be like that with everybody who worked in the business or financial aspects of our lives. Managers, agents, lawyers and accountants: all of them were treated with a level of scepticism until that particular person had proved themselves sufficiently competent and committed, sometimes several times over. Failure, or a misunderstanding of the smaller details, often resulted in a scathing reproach. And from the off, Simon and Jazz had a very big job on their hands.

As far as we were concerned, it was down to them to free us from Innervision. And they had to do it fast.

As *Fantastic* slowly took shape throughout 1982 and 1983, there were other decisions to be made. Wham! was a band big on ambition and George and I were clear on our objective. Top of the list was a number 1 album, both in the UK and America – the latter being essential if we were to become the biggest pop band on the planet. (Another thing on the 'to do' list . . .) We wanted to tour the world and play shows as far away as Australia and the Far East. And it was also important to us that we were playing arenas and maybe even headlining stadiums. Adding pressure to this was a self-imposed deadline. Both George and I knew that the music we were making was driven by teen-age exuberance; it distilled the energy of youth and optimism. Wham! wasn't a band we ever intended to evolve or mature. We wanted to be a short-term sensation, a name that burned brightly and briefly – a few years, maybe – before leaving with a bang. Neither of us wanted Wham! to overstay its welcome and we'd decided that once our targets had been achieved we would bring it to an end. No encores, no comebacks.

But there had been another decision made behind the scenes, of much greater immediate significance for me: in an attempt to accelerate the effort to achieve our goals, George was to take over all songwriting

duties. I'd loved making music and sketching out songs with my best friend, but there was a marked difference between the two of us. I was able to craft chord structures, compose melodies and develop lyrical ideas, as was evidenced by 'Wham Rap', 'Careless Whisper' and 'Club Tropicana', but George was suddenly moving at light speeds. As the great Steve Martin said: 'Some people have a way with words, and other people . . . oh, uh, not have way.' George was firmly in the former camp. Despite his dislike for 'Bad Boys', the way he'd shaped its lyrics and hooks had been impressive. I clearly couldn't match him. Both of us sensed that if Wham! was to have a shot at hitting our targets I'd have to step aside. Neither of us discussed it at first and George later admitted he hadn't wanted to shut me out of the creative process entirely. But a tension was slowly building in and out of the studio to the point where it was clear we needed to talk. One day, we met at my parents' house and, after discussing it, decided that he should write everything. I could only agree that it was the best way for Wham! to make that number 1 record we wanted, and it was a relief to get it out in the open and to have made a decision. The pressure was undoubtedly now heaped upon his shoulders, but we both knew it was for the best.

'Club Tropicana' was going to be our next single. It was a massive departure from everything we'd released before, in terms of style and content, but continuing down the 'Wham Rap', 'Young Guns' route felt like a dead end to us, as George's frustration with 'Bad Boys' illustrated. Beyond that, though, we were unsure of what to record next. We'd been working on two tracks called 'Golden Boy' and 'Soul Boy', but neither of them were any good. With George free to work alone, those choices could happen more freely. Sadly my time as a songwriter was over.

It was the right decision for the band, but I couldn't help but have some second thoughts about it later.

It's a moot point whether or not, at the age of twenty, retirement from making music had been a little too hasty. After all, it wasn't as if I'd been a complete dunce when it came to making records. I'd co-written 'Club Tropicana', 'Wham Rap' and 'Careless Whisper', all of which were huge hits. I also enjoyed the creative process. There was real satisfaction and pleasure to be had in bringing a pop song to life. In retrospect, perhaps what I should have done was step back when the pressure was on in the studio, while working away on my own material in the background. My writing had been integral at the outset; there was no real reason I couldn't have made a contribution again. Nevertheless, I took the view that my prospects of writing a song that would merit inclusion on a Wham! album were pretty slim, and consequently gave up on songwriting completely. I just felt there was absolutely no point in offering up anything to George when he was producing such exceptional material. George was already a very good songwriter and would go on to become a great one. That didn't stop our decision being one that I found hard.

With the writing duties handed over, I can't pretend that my focus on Wham! didn't start to wane. Not to the point where I lost heart in the band, but it wasn't the same. And yet while I was frustrated for sure, songwriting was never the calling for me as it now so clearly was for George. It seemed to have become the vehicle through which he could draw out the person he wanted to be. I knew exactly who I was. I'd set a goal for myself, which was to make a worldwide success of our band, and I was living that ambition. Nevertheless, I still felt envious of George's prodigious talent – I was amazed by it and I admired him immensely for his creative ability. Sure, it would have been fabulous to have some of that stardust sprinkled upon me, but he was also my friend and it was a pleasure and a privilege to see him begin to make the most of his abilities.

Free of any creative pressure, I started to enjoy my new life in the limelight more and more. I partied fairly hard, though not as hard as some people would later suggest. George sometimes painted me as a hellraiser, a sex machine lurching from nightclub to nightclub who slept with any woman. And while I can't deny that there was a little truth in that, I was a lot more restrained than the larger-than-life character exaggerated by George. After the success of our early singles, when we went to the Camden Palace and the Wag Club we were usually photographed drinking and dancing with the likes of Spandau Ballet, Duran Duran and Bananarama. We were afforded entry into the coolest places because of our reputation alone, skipping the long queues whenever we arrived. I got drunk and sometimes messed around but there were never any stories of us getting into bar brawls or trashing hotel rooms. I was just having a good time, but I also knew there was a time and a place for hedonism. We had an album to finish and promotion to do. None of that was going to be completed if I was rolling out of bars at five in the morning.

When *Fantastic* was eventually finished and released on 9 July 1983 it was everything we'd hoped for. The

Left: Downtime in China.

Above: Those hats!

Left: Please not the jumper again!

Above: Those limousines were ancient even in 1983!

Left: Amused by some silliness or other.

Below: An English-man abroad.

Above: 'George! Andy! Would you do some shots with the caps on?'

Below: The Ambassador's Residence, Beijing. And judging by the miserable fizzogs, evidently no Ferrero Rocher!

Right: The Great Wall of
China. Again.
Q: How many times could
the world's press take the
same photo?
A: Until they couldn't.

Below right: Yog barely
concealing his mirth at my
preposterous address at the
welcome banquet given by
the Communist Youth
League.

Below left: Wham! in China
– in case you were in any
doubt!

Top: Poseurs

Bottom left: Prancers

Bottom right: Prats

Above and right: I loved touring.

Below: Celebrating our first No. 1, 'Wake Me Up Before You Go-Go' at George's father, Jack's, restaurant The Angus Pride in Edgware, 1984. That's George's mum behind us in the black Wham! T-shirt, and my mum second from right.

Above and below: On location in Miami for the 'Careless Whisper' video shoot in 1984.

Left: Another bloody photo shoot!

Above: And another . . .

Below: Yep, a bra . . .

album went to number 1 and stayed there for a fort-
night, eventually remaining in the charts for 116 weeks.
Ultimately it was a record of four singles. It's impossible
not to admit that the rest was filler. So unmemorable
were some of the other tracks on the album that even
I struggle to recall their names! But as an opening-shot
release it had served its purpose. *Fantastic* had placed
the songwriting talents of George Michael on the map
while showcasing Wham! as a pop phenomenon in the
making. And with our next single, we were planning a
makeover that we hoped would strike a chord around
the world. 'Club Tropicana' was set for release and with
it a video that would redefine the band.

From now on, we would be impossible to ignore.

14. Revelations

The eighties were the dawn of a new era: the pop video had arrived and with it a generation defining splurge of cinematic ambition. Outrageous production budgets were lavished on pop and rock stars to produce their three-minute masterpieces for MTV. Those customers lucky enough to own the NASA-style satellite dish in their garden were soon treated to the sight of Duran Duran cavorting through a Sri Lankan jungle wearing safari suits. But Saturday morning telly was primed to showcase them too. Kids tuning in to *Saturday Superstore*, or *Swap Shop*, were bombarded with ambitious videos from the likes of Michael Jackson, Cyndi Lauper and Billy Idol. If Wham! was to become one of the biggest bands on the planet, we would have to get in on the act.

'Club Tropicana' was perfectly suited to such an ambitious adventure. It had none of the pomposity of the too-cool-for-school dance-floor scene in London, offering a sort of fantasy teenage summer holiday instead. It was a world away from the rough-around-the-edges mood of the earlier singles. To anyone paying attention, it was clear that George and I didn't take ourselves too seriously. And this sense of fun and escapism would propel us into the Premier League.

When Simon and Jazz announced they had somehow squeezed the budget out of Innervision for Wham! to film the video for 'Club Tropicana' in Ibiza, I was thrilled. Neither of us had been to Ibiza before and it was still a relatively under-the-radar destination for Brits of our age. The Balearic and acid-house scenes that would come to define club culture at the close of the decade were still in their infancy and Ibiza wasn't yet on the circuit of Club 18–30 holidays. Like the song itself, the video storyboard was unlike anything we'd done before. The first half of 'Wham Rap' was filmed in a modest, two-bedroomed terraced house with a young man being told to get a job, or get out. 'Club Tropicana' traded in sunshine, cocktails, pool parties and very skimpy swimming costumes.

The plot, if you could call it that, focused on two young lads enjoying a stay at a boutique Mediterranean hotel alongside Europe's beautiful people. It helped that the location for much of the filming was Pikes Hotel, a luxurious get-away in the north-west corner of the island famously patronised by the likes of Elton John and Freddie Mercury, who later held his infamous forty-first birthday there, when 350 bottles of Moët

In Ibiza for the recording of 'Club Tropicana'.

& Chandon champagne were guzzled beneath a fire-works display so extravagant it could be viewed as far away as Majorca. It was perfect.

The video captured everything George and I imag-ined when we wrote the song in my parents' living room, but had never seen for real. Pikes was so sophis-ticated and swish. Before the shoot, Simon, George and I had dinner on the roof terrace . As the sun went down, cicadas clicked and buzzed in the background. We drank Marqués de Murrieta, a white Rioja that cast the sweet white wine my dad bought in Sainsbury's in a whole new light. Oh, crikey, I thought as I sipped a bit. Now this is more like it . . . George and I must have been twenty years younger than any of the other resi-dents, but we had earned the right to be there. There was every reason to celebrate.

I was woken the morning after we finished the shoot by the telephone ringing loudly by my bed – it was George.

'Hi, Andy . . . Do you want to come over for a quick chat?' he said. I looked at my clock. It was late morning and with nothing on the agenda for the day I assumed we were going to discuss breakfast, or our plans for the coming forty-eight hours. (We'd decided to stay on the island so we could relax for a while.) When I walked across the hallway to George's room, Shirlie was already there, perched on a large sofa in the suite; George was still in bed. He smiled as I came in.

The mood in the room was so relaxed and so familiar, yet what George was about to reveal was clearly a big deal for him.

'I didn't know whether to tell you this . . .' he said, looking across at Shirlie.

'*Go on . . .*'

'. . . but I'm going to: I'm gay.'

I'm not sure whether George was expecting me to react negatively, or if he'd imagined that I'd be shocked or disappointed, but I later learned that he'd confided in Shirlie first. I guess he was looking for reassurance from her that I would be OK. Shirlie knew me better than most, though, and she'd quickly put his mind to rest.

'What are you on?' She'd told him. 'Of course he's going to be fine, he's your best friend. Don't be so silly . . .'

She was right, too. I *was* his best friend. Of course I was fine. Nothing about George's sexuality bothered me in the slightest. I wanted him to be happy.

'Oh, OK.' I shrugged. 'Well, that's a bit of a surprise!'

George then explained it was something that had been on his mind a while. Having arrived in Ibiza he'd met a couple of blokes from Barnsley who I assumed were gay by the way he talked about them afterwards.

'Though I'm not sure whether I'm gay, or bisexual,' he added later.

Having told me the news, he definitely seemed more

relaxed, probably because he realised that it had made absolutely no difference to me whatsoever. In situations like that people often feel the need to crack a joke or two, to dispel any awkwardness, but there really wasn't a heaviness to negotiate. George seemed happy with his announcement. Shirlie and I couldn't have cared less and the three of us went to breakfast as if nothing had happened. And, in truth, it hadn't. For three very close friends it was business as usual.

That George's revelation was soon far from my mind was probably a better indication of the true nature of our friendship than any amount of interrogation or discussion. We were very close in so many ways but relationships, love and heartbreak just never came up. We could talk about music and comedy, happily debating new bands and TV sketches for hours, our conversation peppered with in-jokes, but we never got into one another's feelings. That's just not what our friendship was about.

Part of me wondered why George hadn't felt he could tell me sooner, but it was really no surprise. When it came to romance, neither of us had *ever* confided in the other.

But after that morning in Pikes, certain aspects of George's life made more sense. I'd sometimes wondered why he hadn't ever found a serious girlfriend. There were of course one or two when he was in the sixth form, but that too remained outside our friendship.

The idea that we would ever double-date seemed completely ludicrous to us both.

There was never any plan to go public about George's sexuality. As far as we were both concerned there was no need. It was a far tougher time to be a gay man than it is today and George sensed that it would only cause him trouble, both professionally and personally. He knew that it was unlikely his dad would be pleased by the news. And he feared his sexuality might prove detrimental to his career at a time when it was just taking off.

The girls that bought our records were drawn to the idea of two blokes having a great time together. 'Bad Boys' and 'Club Tropicana' had each sold over four hundred thousand copies; 'Wham Rap!' shifted over a quarter of a million singles. And while the large numbers suggested our audience extended beyond the teen market, George was acutely conscious of how our image contributed to our success. He decided that coming out wasn't a risk he could take. He wanted to become one of the world's greatest artists and his private life wasn't going to be a part of the discussion. For now, everything would have to be kept under wraps.

Musically, George wasn't standing still. He was keen to make a definitive recording of 'Careless Whisper'. He had already recorded a full demo version of the song for Innervision, and the label had attempted to release it, but Dick Leahy stopped them. Now, with *Fantastic* riding high in the charts, George believed the time was right to advance his ambitions as a songwriter. With its more grown-up themes, swooping sax and irresistible chorus, a new and improved version of 'Careless Whisper' could do just that.

Then Dick Leahy presented George with an interesting idea: Why don't you record 'Careless Whisper' at Muscle Shoals in Alabama? Given George's love of classic Atlanta soul, the legendary studio where so much of it had been recorded looked like an inspired choice. Anyone who was anyone had recorded there, including greats like Otis Redding, Wilson Pickett, Aretha Franklin, Paul Simon and the Stones. Meanwhile, Muscle Shoals's in-house producer, Jerry Wexler, and his backing band of session musicians were regarded as some of the best in the business. George jumped at the chance.

Oh my God, thought George as he sat through take after take trying to explain what he was after, these guys are the best, but they're just not getting it.

Played perfectly, George's lilting, heart-bruised melody felt flat and soulless. The realisation unsettled him and when he returned home with the master tape I could tell something was wrong. Initially he kept those thoughts to himself.

He had such huge respect for Wexler. His track record spoke for itself, but perhaps herein lay the problem. A little in awe of the great man, George had taken something of a back seat and allowed Wexler to run the show. The trouble was that however polished a recording Wexler and his band delivered, it would never match the very clear vision George had of the song.

Two different session men were flown in from LA and New York to try to capture the song's signature saxophone intro. Without success. Neither was able to nail the phrasing that made the song so memorable. To really drift over the backing track, the sax part needed to be played fractionally ahead of the beat.

George sat me down in one of our management team's offices. 'What do you think of this, Andy?' he said as he put the Muscle Shoals recording on the stereo.

I listened closely, my heart sinking. All the magic of our original demo had been polished away; the new take was lifeless. I sensed George was waiting for my verdict before voicing his own frustrations.

Even though our songwriting partnership had effectively been dissolved, I owed it to him to give him my honest thoughts on what he'd recorded. George still valued my opinions and we were both quite prepared to ditch an idea if we felt it wasn't working. Glam-rock infused 'Wham! Shake', a demo we'd been wrestling with, was shelved around the same time. 'Careless Whisper', though, was supposed to be George's masterpiece. The last chords of the new recording faded out.

'Well, it's nowhere near as good as the demo, is it?' I said eventually.

15. Soul Boy (Let's Hit The Town)

With the album doing well it was time to go on the road, though I was unsure of exactly what to expect from Wham!'s first UK tour. That run of limited public appearances using a backing track meant that our experience of performing was fairly limited. Despite this, I was quite relaxed about what was shaping up to be a thirty-date tour. *Aberdeen, Edinburgh, Glasgow.* Playing live had been one of my ambitions ever since George and I had formed the Executive as a pair of sixteen-year-old kids. *Leicester, St Austell, Bristol.* And a proper UK tour meant an opportunity to play songs conceived by me and George in living rooms and bedrooms in front of real, live, paying audiences. *London, Whitley Bay, Poole.* I was looking forward to what promised to be the pop equivalent of an Enid Blyton novel. An adventure featuring four (fairly) innocent twenty-something kids. *Swansea, Birmingham, Brighton.*

Four Go Touring.

For George, however, the prospect of performing

WHAM!

OCTOBER 1983

Mon	10th	ABERDEEN Capitol Theatre	£5.00 £4.50 £4.00
Tues	11th	EDINBURGH Playhouse Theatre	£5.00 £4.50 £4.00
Thurs	13th	GLASGOW Apollo Theatre	£5.00 £4.50 £4.00
Fri	14th	LANCASTER University	£4.00
Sat	15th	NEWCASTLE City Hall	£5.00 £4.50 £4.00
Sun	16th	MANCHESTER Apollo	£5.00 £4.50 £4.00
Tues	18th	LIVERPOOL Royal Court Theatre	£5.00 £4.50 £4.00
Wed	19th	SHEFFIELD City Hall	£5.00 £4.50 £4.00
Fri	21st	LEICESTER De Montfort Hall	£5.00 £4.50 £4.00
Sat	22nd	ST AUSTELL Coliseum	£5.00 £4.50 £4.00
Sun	23rd	BRISTOL Studio	£5.00
Mon	24th	SWANSEA Top Rank	£5.00
Thur	27th	HAMMERSMITH Odeon	£5.00 £4.50 £4.00
Sun	30th	BRIGHTON Centre	£5.00 £4.50 £4.00

NOVEMBER 1983

Tues	1st	NOTTINGHAM Royal Court Theatre	£5.00 £4.50 £4.00
Wed	2nd	POOLE Arts Centre	£5.00 £4.50 £4.00
Thurs	3rd	CRAWLEY Leisure Centre	£5.00
Fri	4th	LEEDS University	£4.25
Sun	6th	BIRMINGHAM Odeon	£5.00 £4.50 £4.00

THE CLUB FANTASTIC
TOUR!

**THEIR NO. 1
ALBUM & CASSETTE**

our songs before a live audience heaped on yet more pressure. With the music press turning nasty following the release of the exuberant 'Club Tropicana', and the tabloids describing us as a heart-throb boy band, he worried that we weren't being taken seriously enough. The Club Fantastic tour was our chance to prove the doubters wrong, but to succeed, everything we played onstage had to be polished and pitch-perfect. Our music and his songwriting had to shine. It had to be fun, for sure, but when it came to taking our musical songbook on the road, the sound and musical arrangements had to be as meticulously locked down as they were in the studio.

While this might have seemed straightforward enough, neither George nor I were under any illusions. Our records hadn't been worked up in rehearsal rooms or live jams. Nothing had been sketched out in the back of a tour bus and allowed to evolve over time. By contrast, George and I had written the likes of 'Wham Rap' then recorded them faithfully. As such, Wham! possessed a set list of songs honed in the studio that had never been played live. We knew we had to incorporate the choreographed dance routines fans had seen on *Top of the Pops* for 'Young Guns' and 'Bad Boys'. It was what they were paying to see, after all. If we didn't incorporate that level of showmanship there was likely to be a fair bit of disappointment and neither of us wanted to underwhelm in any way.

We also had to faithfully reproduce the songs as they had been recorded. Wham! was hardly cut from the same cloth as Genesis, Pink Floyd or Emerson, Lake & Palmer and there would be no room for extended grooves or improvised solos. We knew that Wham! fans wanted to hear the hits, played loud, just as they sounded on the radio. There was no room for self-indulgence.

Despite George's concerns about whether the music was afforded sufficient respect, the show had to reflect the band's youthful energy and sense of fun. 'Club Tropicana' was pure hedonism, so the leather and denim of 'Young Guns' was out. Instead I pushed the sportswear look. It would better capture the sense of freedom and escapism that we wanted our audience to enjoy.

To help reinforce the party atmosphere, we decided that, instead of a support band, we'd use Capital Radio DJ Gary Crowley as our warm-up act. Gary had been one of the first DJs to push Wham! so his inclusion felt fitting. To complete the clubby, block-party vibe, we had breakdance group Eklypse perform during Gary's set. The whole Club Fantastic concept was squarely aimed at Wham!'s young female fans. Any disgruntled brothers and boyfriends dragged along for the ride would just have to take whatever they could from it all.

A glimpse of what awaited us came a few weeks before the tour's opening night. Wham! had been invited to perform at Capital Radio's Best Disco in Town show at the Lyceum Theatre in London. This was the first time we had performed in anything close to a genuine live setting. Those early club PAs had done little to prepare us for it. As soon as we walked onstage a barrage of screams ricocheted around the auditorium. The whole place was crammed with shrieking girls waving banners and flags and screaming. You felt it as much as you heard it. A teddy was thrown onstage. Then what looked like a bra. I glanced across at George in disbelief.

'Bloody hell,' I shouted over the din. 'I wasn't expecting this!'

But what were we expecting, really? 'Club Tropicana' had ignited the public's imagination in a way we could scarcely have dreamt of. And in the background our manager, Simon, was fanning the flames. Having wined and dined the showbiz editors of every single newspaper in the country, Simon ensured our names were being emblazoned across the nation's pages on a daily basis. The column inches lavished on us seemed extraordinary, even in an industry renowned for generating hyperbole. It quickly became a full-time job just to separate fact from fantasy. The majority of headlines definitely fell in the latter camp and, as if there was ever any doubt, it mostly confirmed the old adage that sex sells.

One such tale 'accidentally' relayed by Simon to the *Evening Standard* suggested that George had suggested our foursome should sleep in the same suite at Pike's Hotel. Inevitably enough, this arrangement led to wild sexual abandon. Simon had spun his story over a long and boozy lunch and later claimed to have regretted it. But by early evening, the Standard was screaming 'Wham! Orgy!' on its front page.

Of course, the story was a complete fabrication, but Simon's view was that it was all grist to the mill. Anything to keep the fans at fever pitch was fine by him. As a band, we realised that being equally cheeky with the press was an excellent tactic for dealing with the monotony of interviews. Neither of us particularly enjoyed the process but, in autumn of 1983, as we prepared for the forthcoming shows, we recognised that we had to play along. Simon knew the promotion game better than anyone and decided the best way to sell tickets was to keep Wham! in the news. As we spoke to a succession of journalists, I came to realise that neither what I said nor how nicely I said it made the slightest difference. The story was that we were a pair of sex-mad boys about to embark on the ride of our lives and nothing we could say or do was going to make them deviate from that.

To amuse ourselves, we concocted stories of our own, fabricating tales of imaginary sexual endeavours that reached preposterous levels, but what was little more than an attempt to alleviate the boredom didn't look so good in print. The comments had been always tongue-in-cheek but, ironically enough given our concerns about how the music was regarded, were treated with altogether too much respect. On one occasion I treated a journalist to the revelation that I was a 'fantastic lover'.

'I like getting to know a girl over a candlelit meal,' I continued. 'If we like each other we go back to her place or to a hotel . . . Now we've become heart-throbs we take great care over our appearance. George climbs on to a sunbed as soon as he gets a little pale and I try not to go the supermarket in my slippers any more.'

What?!

My attempt at irreverent humour ended up landing very wide of the mark, but that didn't stop it being used to fill pages and pages of newsprint. My quotes were blown up in big letters underneath the headline:

'Wham Bam!' In the accompanying photographs, taken as part of the 'Club Tropicana' photo shoot, the pair of us lounged seductively in too-tight board shorts.

George and I would laugh in disbelief as we read the morning papers. It was ludicrous.

But as a promotional tool, however, Simon's strategy worked magnificently well. At the box office, the Club Fantastic tour was a sell-out success.

Whamania had started.

16. The Teenage Fan Club

On the night of our first show at the Capitol Theatre in Aberdeen, the pair of us had been extremely excited as we waited in our dressing room for stage time. Neither of us had been able to sit still and we'd bounced around the room at the thought of playing our first proper headline gig. We were not the only ones.

Once our road trip got under way, running through Aberdeen, Edinburgh and Glasgow, the hype and hysteria enveloped us as we went. Onstage we did everything we could to stoke it, the pair of us happily flirting with our newfound playboy image. To help finance the tour, Simon and Jazz had somehow secured a deal with the sports brand Fila, most famous for kitting out a raft of tennis stars in their Wimbledon whites. Unfortunately, the clobber, when it arrived in bright shades of red and yellow, bordered on the ridiculous. Slim-fitting tracksuit bottoms were offset by Wham! crop tops and sporty jackets, which we planned to swap around during a series of costume changes. But it was the shorts that everyone remembers. They looked more like hot pants. George and I more or less got away with it, but our sartorial choices did not go down so well with some members of the backing band.

The idea of playing around with a sporty image in our crop tops and shorts seemed like harmless fun, but typically we pushed the humour as far as we felt we could. And the temperature among our young female fans really sizzled whenever George whipped a shuttlecock from his pocket, then ran it teasingly up and down his arms before dropping it into his shorts. Oh, bloody hell . . . *no*, I thought during the first night on the road as George then fished it out and flicked it into the front rows. I watched incredulously every night as thousands of teenage girls lost their minds at this unusual mass-seduction technique. At times it was hard to comprehend what was happening.

God knows what my poor parents are going to make of it, I wondered before they came to watch us perform. Dad, it turned out, was totally bemused by the whole affair as his son's contribution to eighties pop was drowned out by several thousand screaming girls. Wham!'s music and its mass appeal remained a complete mystery to him; he was simply unable to comprehend how two twenty-year-old boys were already enjoying the same sort of commercial success as some of the biggest bands from his own teenage years. Once she'd got over the initial shock, Mum seemed to love it and told

me how proud she was of our success. But Mum was only forty herself. The idea of her son playing sold-out gigs to crowds of crazed pop fans must have seemed unbelievable.

It seemed pretty unbelievable from where we were standing too. Of course, the screaming and crying was endlessly flattering. Whamania had nothing to do with critical acclaim but that didn't matter to me – not next to the adoration we were given by the audience. The kids screaming at us every night were *our* fans, *our* audience, and so we had huge affection for them. I was just grateful that they adored Wham!. I never fell into the trap of thinking, Oh my God, I'm suddenly *really* attractive to women. *But there was no denying it was still a bit of a rush.*

The mood was no less crazy away from the stage. As soon as we'd finished our encore – often a cover of Chic's 'Good Times' – we'd try to escape via the stage door before the crowds surrounded us. We rarely beat them, though. And even from the safety of the car it was unnerving. We'd be thrown around inside as it swayed from side to side, at the mercy of a crush of teenage girls. Hands clawed at the locked doors. Fists pounded on the windows. Dozens of faces pressed against the glass. Oh come on, girls, I'd think, looking out at the madness as it seemed to seethe around our ride. Calm down, just for a moment. *Please* . . .

More than anything I remember the shouting and

frenzy, a deafening cacophony that, on one occasion, was interrupted by the dull thud of a girl breaking free from the crowd and sprawling across the car bonnet. She crawled towards us, mouthing our names. *'George!'* Her limbs flailed like an extra from a George Romero zombie movie. *'Andrew!'*

When I glanced across at George, I sensed a wave of anxiety. He was stressed by the bewildering situation we were in and concerned that somebody might get seriously hurt as two tons of steel inched edged forward into a sea of screaming, crying, waving teenage flesh.

Our driver pressed his hand against the horn and kept it there. The wall of faces, suddenly aware that they might find themselves crushed beneath our wheels, took a collective step backwards, then two, as we edged away.

Only once the car had gathered enough speed for the pack to recede in our rear-view mirror did we begin to relax. But we weren't out of the woods yet. While most of the girls were left in our wake, hugging, crying and screaming, the lunatic fringe gave chase and ran towards the incoming traffic, darting across busy streets to risk their necks for another glimpse of me and George as we laughed nervously in the back. The mood was *crazed*.

And exactly the response our management team had hoped for.

Despite the female attention heaped upon us, life on the road was hardly sex, drugs and rock'n'roll. Shirlie was a good friend of both of us. We'd been joined by a new singer, Helen DeMacque, known as 'Pepsi', after Dee decided to join Paul Weller's band, the Style Council, but despite the arrival of a new face, the vibe backstage remained as happy and uncomplicated as ever. There was nothing of the last-gang-in-town mentality that was inextricably linked to hard-living rock acts like Motörhead or Aerosmith. And despite the odd impromptu toga party on that first tour, any carrying on with fans was definitely off the agenda.

Given that our audience was largely made up of pre-pubescent girls and reluctant chaperones, George and I looked elsewhere for company. Despite his announcement in Ibiza, George's private life remained closed to the rest of the group and the public. That was nothing new. George had always operated discreetly and wasn't about to start announcing the details of any conquests he might have made on tour. He also felt that when we were together, the pair of us attracted too much attention. With all eyes were trained on us it was impossible for him to enjoy any privacy. Alone, George could play a little faster and looser with his love life, and within London's gay and club scene, in venues such as Mud Club and the Wag, his true sexuality was slowly emerging. Outside of a very small, trusted circle George remained careful, though. He didn't make passes at

 WHAM!

No Unauthorised Entry

GEORGE, ANDREW, SHIRLIE + PEPSI

men when the attention was on Wham!, still fearing that being outed might spell career disaster, even in an industry where the concept of sexuality was becoming increasingly fluid.

The opportunities for sexual indulgence were actually few and far between for either of us. The myth suggests an easy life with the occasional smattering of intense activity – a show here, a glamorous photo shoot there – to fill the empty hours. The reality was very different for Wham! A busy schedule of radio, press and TV interviews on that first tour meant there simply wasn't the time to play around, not that either of us were too bothered. Nor did I pine after emotional support or affection. George and I relied on each other, but we were also young and surrounded by friends like Pepsi and Shirlie. We became a tight social circle with a close, happy family vibe to it. Throwing random girls into the mix on a nightly basis would have been an odd thing to do.

We were unerring in our focus on making a success of Wham!.

And then disaster struck.

George's voice took a hammering every night as he sang and joked around for ninety minutes at a time. By the end of October and with around half the tour completed, his vocal cords started to give out and it became clear that he was unable to continue.

'I'm sorry, Andrew,' he said after he'd struggled through the first of two London dates. 'We might have to put off the tour for a bit – what do you think?'

I nodded, though the thought of cancelling was horrifying. I'd been having a whale of a time and was eager to press on, but I also knew that if the strain was so bad that George was suggesting we postpone the forthcoming shows, well, it must have been pretty serious. He certainly wasn't one to make excuses and no one grasped the importance of our first tour more than him. But George wasn't going to make the decision alone. He seemed so sure of himself when it came to making music, but he still needed reassurance when it came to settling big questions. Invariably, he looked to me for confirmation in situations like this.

He knew I saw the world in much the same way he did and, most importantly, that my view would always be informed by our friendship rather than any outside influence. Neither of us expected anything less of the other.

Even before he began struggling with his voice, I sensed that George wasn't as keen on touring as I was. So much of how he'd defined himself was wrapped up in his songwriting. In the studio he was in control. Out of it, on tour, there were too many variables to deal with – and too much that might go wrong. This stressed him out. If he wasn't in his hotel room, or fulfilling a promotional commitment, George was often found at the venue, ensuring every detail of our live show was as perfect as it could be. Our sound had to be absolutely spot-on. He had an incredible ear, picking up glitches and flaws that were beyond the range of most people. If there was an issue with a microphone or stage monitor, he had the confidence to call it, even if his was a lone voice. And he always called it right.

His attention to detail was well rewarded, though. The Club Fantastic tour was a sell-out success; our debut album had been a massive hit. But, while I was happy just being part of a touring pop act and revelling in our exploding popularity, George needed more. *This was only just his beginning.* Once he'd realised that musical success of the kind being enjoyed in 1983 by the likes of David Bowie, Michael Jackson or Billy Joel was within Wham!'s grasp, his determination and confidence grew exponentially. There was only one question on his mind: *How quickly can we get there?* The next hit, the next affirmation of his ability became a priority.

My life was a lot more straightforward. I was living in the moment and wasn't too fussed about how long the adventure might last for, or what Wham!'s legacy might be. But then I never felt that our music defined me in the same way it did him. Simply *being* in Wham! meant that I'd already reached the summit of my musical ambition.

I was also more than happy to be roaming around the country in a tour bus with what was proving to be a

merry gang. By contrast, George's attachment to home and family life was far more deep-rooted. It had a lot to do with the distinct public and private aspects of his personality. At home he could be Georgios, Yog, *himself*, and the stability that brought him was important. While on tour, working with Wham!, George was presenting a public image that didn't come naturally to him.

If ever we were staying in a hotel he preferred to remain in his bedroom where he was undisturbed by the fans gathered outside. He was rarely excited by the places we travelled to; they held no interest for him. Nor do I think he really enjoyed the repetitive nature of performing the same material over and over, night after night. It quickly became a chore to him. Whether writing songs or recording, George was much happier creating and crafting new material. To cap it all, when we played live, there was always a lot more pressure on him to be the showman than there ever was on me. Onstage, I was able to move in and out of focus.

And I didn't have to sing.

The initial umming and ahing regarding what to do about George's voice and the rest of the tour made us miserable. There was, for a while, pressure for us to push on regardless. But George held his ground in the face of promoters and management attempting to twist his arm and the tour was postponed, giving him a chance to recuperate.

But the fact that his voice, *his instrument*, had failed at such a vital moment was a major concern. George wasn't one to run through scales in a pre-show warm-up routine, or sip larynx-soothing cups of honey and lemon before bed. We hadn't known at the time that George had polyps in his throat, which would later require surgery. On the Club Fantastic tour, the cause of his croaking voice remained a mystery and a somewhat unnerving one.

With the remaining dates rescheduled for the end of the year, I returned home to my parents' house. I was riding high with one of the breakout albums of the year and a sell-out UK tour, my face splashed across the front of every single tabloid and magazine in the country – but I was still skint. We were still some way from Jazz and Simon successfully disentangling us from our record contract with Innervision, but as I lay in my cramped bedroom I wasn't too fussed. Like George I had a sense of where we were both heading. There would be plenty more adventures to come.

Fans frequently turned up on the doorstep, but Mum always welcomed them with a smile.

17. Fun and Games

Once George's voice had recovered, the remainder of the tour sizzled to its conclusion to the sound of screaming girls. At the same time, true to their word, Jazz and Simon managed to free us from our contract with Innervision.

As a parting slap in the face, the label released the ghastly *Club Fantastic Megamix*, a medley of the hits so far, without our consent. We could do nothing to stop it, but they would get no more from Wham!. We signed a new deal with Epic Records in the UK and Columbia in the US. And, looking forward to being more fairly rewarded for our efforts, we began thinking about the new record.

George had the songs to make swift work of the creative process and quickly recorded the first single, making use of studio time originally booked to record the aborted 'Wham Shake!' The new song's lyrical inspiration came from an unlikely source: a note I'd stuck to my parents' fridge before going to bed. It read, 'Mum, wake me up up before you go go.'

From little acorns . . .

Quite what, as a twenty-year-old pop star, I needed to get up for remains a mystery. What caused me to double up on ups and gos is easier to guess at. But the note caught George's eye, triggering thoughts of the effervescent rock'n'roll records of the fifties and sixties. The song that followed captured it all and more. From the jitterbug and finger-snapping that announced its arrival, every part of 'Wake Me Up Before You Go-Go' fizzed with fun and energy. Its infectious melody, relentless bounce and sing-along chorus were irresistible. With 'Wake Me Up' under our belts, the new album had its opening track. Next up was the song that ended up closing the album: 'Careless Whisper'.

After giving up on the Muscle Shoals recording, George booked himself into SARM West Studios in London with an engineer in early 1984. We had lived with that song for three years now and both of us understood how it needed to sound. Now, installed in a studio and free of any outside influence, George got to work on trying to finally capture that. When he finally emerged from SARM with the finished master tape, the new recording of 'Careless Whisper' carried all the sparkle of the original and more. Much more. After hiring and firing ten different sax players, George eventually heard what he was looking for from number eleven. At last, the nuanced melody that had lived inside his head for so long found expression from a saxophonist with soul and sensibility as well as virtuosity.

The recording was definitive. One of those rare classics that has been covered by a myriad of artists as diverse as Gloria Gaynor and alternative metal band Seether. George had recorded his first masterpiece and nobody was more pleased about that than I was. 'Careless Whisper' was a song we'd written together.

In the wake of his passing it's been suggested that George gave me a co-writing credit as an act of generosity, the implication being that I *couldn't* have helped him with the writing. That misunderstands the nature of our relationship at Wham!'s inception. It goes without saying that when it came to musical talent, George was in a completely different league to me – as he was to most people! But in those early days we bounced

ideas off each other without even knowing we were doing it. I was a sounding board and a creative sidekick who shared an instinctive understanding with George. The creation of 'Careless Whisper' was inextricably linked to our shared experience. We were so close that it was never much of a surprise to either of us when we arrived at the same idea completely independently of each other. It would have been a whole lot weirder if we hadn't been so in tune with each other's thinking. By the time we wrote 'Careless Whisper' we communicated almost exclusively through shared jokes, knowing references and comedy quotes. So much so that Simon characterised our relationship in terms of Butch Cassidy and the Sundance Kid.

But now, as close as our bond remained, the nature of the relationship was changing. I found myself in an unusual position. Our decision to defer to him completely for the songwriting meant I was out on something of a limb. As George began to gather material for our second album, part of me began to rue the fact that I no longer had the same involvement in the creation of the music as I'd once enjoyed. I understood why and I had readily and happily agreed to it, but I missed the fun and bonhomie of thrashing out melodies, lyrics and arrangements with George. The thought of simply being famous for being in Wham! didn't appeal. Despite what some of the papers were saying – and it was becoming an increasing source of sport for them – I loved making music and performing. With any opportunity for the former now stripped away, it was hard to avoid becoming a target for the press, who poked fun at my lack of involvement in the band. While George threw himself into writing and recording, I became a lightning rod for media interest in Wham!.

With no reason not to I went out more and more and my reputation as a party animal and hellraiser gathered momentum. Along the way, headlines like 'Randy Andy' and 'Animal Andy' attached themselves to me. Newspaper editors seemed to revel in presenting me as a slightly wayward character, but in reality I was really behaving no differently to how any other 21-year-old might have done in the circumstances. I liked hanging out with friends over a beer or two. And, after breaking up with Shirlie, I was able to play the field without ever really settling into a relationship. Not that there was actually much time to have a serious girlfriend. With Wham! going global that meant promotional appearances, photo shoots and tours around the world. The result was that there were a number of fun, fleeting encounters throughout that period of my life. The acres of newsprint they seemed to generate in their wake usually enjoyed only the loosest relationship with the truth. It was often hilarious, too.

With 'Wake Me Up' and 'Careless Whisper' in the can it was decided we should record the rest of the album in the South of France at the same studio where Pink Floyd had put the finishing touches to *The Wall*. Studio Miraval was hidden away within acres of vineyards and so peace and quiet, away from the media spotlight in London, was guaranteed.

From the moment I first joined him in France, I was impressed by George's optimism about the next record, which we were calling *Make It Big*. He was in a good place, fully immersed in the studio environment and happy to be in complete control of the creative process.

George was blossoming as a songwriter. And at such a rapid rate too. The leap from 'Wham Rap!' to 'Young

Guns' had seemed dramatic at the time, but by the time George was writing *Make it Big*, those early hits were already starting to sound dated. 'Club Tropicana' had broken the mould at exactly the right moment, though, allowing us to approach the next album with a new creative freedom. We'd been pushing out the boundaries with the first few singles, but now, as far as George was concerned, the shackles were off.

What excited him most was the prospect of exploring themes on *Make It Big* that would help propel him towards his solo career. While the new songs were immediately catchy and effervescent, the lyrics were becoming more sophisticated and mature. 'Everything She Wants' had a seriousness and depth that would have been unimaginable when we worked up those first early Wham! demos. A wry commentary on the challenges of young married life, it was shot through with wit and insight. Over a pumping funk bass line finely turned lines like 'If my best isn't good enough, then how can it be good enough for two?' or 'And now you tell me that you're having my baby, I'll tell you that I'm happy if you want me to', were evidence that George was now writing for an audience that was older, wiser and more careworn than the Whamania-crazed kids that had fallen for *Fantastic*.

Whenever he finished a new track it was usually played back at full blast. He was particularly excited about 'Freedom' and couldn't wait to play me the rough

mix he'd been working on. Although my own contribution to the creative process was now limited to
playing the guitar and providing backing vocals,
George still sought my opinion as confirmation of his
thoughts and I was only too happy to provide a little
input whenever needed. And it was while listening to
'Freedom' that I probably first considered George's
lyrics in the context of his sexuality. We'd recorded *Fantastic* before he confided in me and Shirlie in Ibiza, and
so I'd always assumed he was writing about girls from
school or the girlfriends he'd had in his late teens. But
when the chorus of 'Freedom' claimed 'Girl, all I want
right now is you' and spoke of 'a prisoner who has his
own key' and a 'lover with another' it did make me
pause.

Hmm, I wonder what this is about? I thought.

Whoever might have inspired the song, George was
keeping their identity shrouded in mystery. What was
beyond doubt, though, was the quality of the songs
themselves.

And any frustration I felt at being sidelined during
the songwriting was balanced by the knowledge that
we would soon be going on tour again, playing the
songs for hundreds of thousands of fans around the
world. I'd come to terms with the division of responsibility, putting aside my personal feelings and accepting
my side of the bargain. With *Make It Big* we were preparing for lift-off. It couldn't come soon enough for

me because the press stories about me were becoming more lurid than ever.

In one memorable 'exclusive' that appeared a little later, two Page Three models were photographed standing either side of a cardboard cutout of me. Published alongside it were paragraphs of nonsense and innuendo. Apparently I'd been two-timing both girls. In the scoop that followed I was described as both a 'super-stud' and a 'rotten Romeo'. They described how I was driven back to my flat by one of the girls. While I stroked her knee and kissed her neck she caressed 'the gearstick . . . of her car'. It was enough to make Jilly Cooper blush. And not a word was true. I'd never met either of them, but we let it go. I understood how the game was supposed to work. Our faces sold newspapers and, in return, that helped sell records and concert tickets.

That didn't mean that while George was out of the spotlight my efforts to keep the band in the public eye were entirely comfortable, nor were they always completely harmless.

Aged nine, I was swimming widths underwater at Wall Hall College, where my mum was undergoing her teacher training, and slammed into the side of the pool. I clambered out in a daze, trailing blood from a broken nose. The operation to widen the airways damaged by the collision was successful, but only partially so.

'When you're twenty-one,' the doctor explained, 'your septum can be straightened out. Your breathing will be much better from then on.' None of us anticipated that, at twenty-one, I would be living through Whamania. I decided to use the time before recording *Make It Big* to undergo the surgery so that I would have time to recover. If the press thought I was going under the knife for a nose job they'd have a field day. Then Simon thought he'd come up with the perfect smokescreen to explain the surgical dressings criss-crossing my face.

While I recovered in hospital, Nomis leaked a story to the press that I'd been the victim of an unfortunate dance-floor calamity.

I'd been at a party, they suggested, when an over-exuberant David Mortimer, who had now changed his name to David Austin, had picked up an ice bucket and started swinging it round his head in a wild dance.

Crack!

I walked unknowingly into his path. My nose took the full brunt of it and had required immediate corrective surgery.

Poor Andrew!

On paper it had all the hallmarks of a Simon classic: alcohol-fuelled high jinks, slapstick comedy and a little pathos. But neither of us had anticipated that David would end up being the real victim. While I convalesced at home, surrounded by cards, flowers and gifts from family, friends and fans, David had become the fall guy. He was bombarded by angry phone calls and abusive letters accusing him of inflicting grievous bodily

From one of Mum's scrapbooks.

harm on me. As the newspapers scented blood, Wham! fans descended on his house threatening revenge. Less than twenty-four hours after the story broke, his mum called me in a fury.

'You should be ashamed of yourself, Andrew,' she told me. 'What a disgraceful thing to have done! Did you have any idea how bad this would be for David?'

And of course we didn't. I'd never felt so chastised in all my life. There really is nothing quite like taking a scolding from a mate's mum. Her son had been burned and now I was getting singed. In the end I had to come clean about what had really happened: I'd had corrective surgery and David had nothing to do with it. The angry mob camping out on his front lawn soon lost interest.

On this occasion, the furore had been self-inflicted, but it did nothing to ease what had become an increasingly fraught relationship between me and the showbiz press.

'Wake Me Up Before You Go-Go' was released in May, crashing into the charts at number 4 before hitting the top spot a week later.

Our first number 1!

George and I were thrilled at the thought of making it to that coveted position, driven by airplay on the same radio shows we'd listened to so avidly as kids. We marked the occasion with a party at Jack's restaurant in Edgware. Even George's dad now realised we'd done

something worth celebrating. With its radio ubiquity and heavy presence in the clubs, 'Wake Me Up' had grown our audience beyond the screaming girls who'd rushed us on the Club Fantastic tour and lent weight to George's loftier ambitions. He'd proved to everybody that he was truly capable of making the Big Hit.

The success of 'Wake Me Up' was helped along by an exuberant video filmed at Brixton Academy in South London in front of several thousand screaming fans. While part of the performance was shot while we cavorted around the stage in the bright colours and short shorts we'd pioneered during the Club Fantastic tour, it was our change of wardrobe for which the video is most often remembered. Against an all-white set, the pair of us wore white T-shirts with 'CHOOSE LIFE' emblazoned across the front in heavy block lettering. Created by fashion designer Katherine Hamnett at a time of heightened Cold War tension when concerns about possible nuclear apocalypse seemed frighteningly real, the slogan was designed as all-encompassing rallying cry against the world's ills. The Buddhism-inspired design had originally been spotted by a friend of George's, who thought it might make for a striking visual image. Political sloganeering certainly wasn't at the forefront of our minds when we decided on them for the 'Wake Me Up' video, but its irresistible incitement to live life to the full made it the perfect choice. It went on to be one of the decade's defining looks. With 'Wake Me Up' providing a soundtrack to summer, it felt as if we were surfing a wave.

Perhaps emboldened by the song's massive success and the realisation that his ideas now had truly broad appeal, George called his next shot.

Well aware of the huge potential of 'Careless Whisper', we'd decided, the previous year, to wait for an opportune moment to release it – one that would give it the best opportunity to shine. With the transatlantic number 1 success of 'Wake Me Up Before You Go-Go', that moment had arrived.

We both knew the song marked a massive departure from the up-tempo rhythms of everything we'd done before and had agreed, prior to the Club Fantastic Tour, that its release required careful handling. In a way, a moody ballad seemed like a radical move for Wham!. Its grown-up themes made it so very different from the rest of our back catalogue, but it was without doubt our best song so far. Alongside songs like 'Wake Me Up' and 'Club Tropicana' it stuck out like a sore thumb. It was also a test for us. We wanted to release it on the same day on both sides of the Atlantic. If we were going to be one of the biggest pop bands on the planet, we had to conquer America.

We'd agreed previously that the song would be released as a solo track for George in the UK, but the song was to be billed as 'Wham! Featuring George Michael' in the US. The thinking behind the move was that while Wham! was huge at home they weren't quite there across the pond. If the band was going to lay the foundations for George's solo career down the line, he needed us to be massive in both territories.

Despite the fact that I'd co-written the song I was quite content with the idea of George releasing it as a solo project: he had taken it to another level in the studio. And we both knew it would open the eyes

of a sceptical minority to what might be possible for George beyond Wham!

Had we not built a limited shelf life into the band's DNA from the outset, I thought that 'Careless Whisper' could have been to us what 'Save A Prayer' was to Duran Duran or 'True' to Spandau Ballet. But I understood George's ambition to become an artist in his own right. He was always going to have to push forward alone at some point. Until that time came, I wanted to make sure that, in resolutely pursuing our mutually held ambition of helping to realise Wham!'s full potential, I'd done all I could to provide him with the springboard he needed.

I told George that I completely supported the idea of him releasing the song as a solo single.

18. Let it Snow, Let it Snow, Let it Snow

Make It Big went straight in at number 1, hitting the top spot not only in Britain but Australia, Holland, Italy, Japan, New Zealand and, after a while, America. Even by the high standards we set ourselves, this was undoubtedly a massive success. *Make It Big* eventually went on to shift around 10 million copies worldwide. By the time of the album's release in October, 'Wake Me Up Before You Go-Go' had been followed to number 1 by 'Careless Whisper' under George's name in July. *Make It Big* included both singles. Alongside global chart success, we were also beginning to enjoy a measure of the critical acclaim we felt was due, but had been a long time coming.

Since the release of 'Careless Whisper', though, people had started to wonder aloud whether the end of Wham! was in sight. They'd speculated that George's first single was a sign that he wanted to break up Wham! and go solo, but while that was very much his long-term goal, they hadn't understood how serious we were about first becoming one of the biggest pop bands on

Nº1 8 DEC

THIS WEEK	LAST WEEK	WEEKS IN CHART	HIGHEST POSITION	U.K. ALBUMS
1	1	4	1	**MAKE IT BIG** Wham (CBS)
2	2	4	2	**ALF** Alison Moyet (CBS)
3	14	2	3	**THE HITS ALBUM** Various (WEA/CBS)
4	4	4	4	**THE COLLECTION** Ultravox (Chrysalis)
5	7	20	1	**DIAMOND LIFE** Sade (CBS)
6	3	5	1	**WELCOME TO THE PLEASURE DOME** Frankie Goes To Hollywood (ZTT)
7	5	14	2	**ELIMINATOR** ZZ Top (Warner Bros)
8	6	3	6	**ARENA** Duran Duran (EMI)
9	—	1	9	**NOW THAT'S WHAT I CALL MUSIC IV** Various (EMI-Virgin)
10	35	2	10	**12 GOLD BARS VOLS I & II** Status Quo (Vertigo)

the planet. As well as number 1 records, we wanted to sell out stadiums. Our plan was to tour the world and, ultimately, conquer America. We wanted to be as big there as we were in Britain and so breaking Wham! apart before achieving that would have been a failure in our eyes. And there was no way George was going to allow Wham! to be tainted by any suggestion of failure. If he was to go solo, he needed Wham! to be as successful as the likes of Duran Duran, Prince or U2.

Of course the rumours weren't entirely wide of the mark. As the success of *Make It Big* unfolded, George was becoming increasingly interested in becoming a solo artist and began to make more and more solo appearances on the TV and radio. I also understood we didn't have long to achieve our ambition. We were a band built

on the idea of youth and exuberance. There was no way we could stay kids forever and I'd always liked the idea of us going out at the top rather than fading away – nobody liked a guest who outstayed their welcome.

Simon and Jazz were also aware of George's plans to disband, though I'm not entirely sure they really believed him. In a couple of interviews he'd mentioned the possibility of us recording a third album together. As shrewd businessmen, they couldn't take the risk of not cashing in on Wham!'s money-making potential while they had the chance. They booked a lucrative arena tour in support of *Make It Big*, but despite the announcement of dates in the UK, Far East, Australia and the States, gossip columnists kept on making guesses about our demise. George, though,

had another trick up his sleeve that might throw them off the scent.

Wham! had recorded a Christmas number-1-in-waiting.

'Last Christmas' began its life one afternoon in 1984 at George's parents' home. As we watched football on the telly, George was suddenly struck by inspiration. He quickly sketched out a chorus and verse on his keyboard upstairs. But with the addition of some tinkling synths and, of course, sleigh bells, George's initially memorable melody had the makings of a festive classic. I only had to listen to the demo once to realise 'Last Christmas' was a huge hit; after George added his bells and whistles in London's Advision Studios, shortly after the recording of *Make It Big*, we set a December

I'm not entirely sure what this added to the show!

release date and waited expectantly. The likes of Slade and John Lennon had already shown that if you were capable of writing a killer Christmas single, it had every chance of becoming a perennial favourite. There was also George's Christmas Eve party to look forward to. George loved Christmas and the previous year he had hosted a gathering that would become a regular fixture for the next few years. After a boozy dinner, all twenty-five guests had gone carol singing, though rather than knocking door to door with charity boxes and hymn sheets, we had taken a blow-up sex doll for company. Not everyone had been amused.

Christmas seemed to bring out the worst in us, as a similar spirit of mischievousness attached itself to the filming of the 'Last Christmas' promo video. Our directors had arranged a shoot in the mountain resort of Saas-Fee in Switzerland that November. In the 1980s, skiing holidays had a distinctly aspirational feel to them and so the idea of filming in a cosy ski chalet, roaring fire and all, felt like the perfect winter companion to the sunny hedonism of 'Club Tropicana', where George and I had spent a couple of glorious days messing about in Ibiza. This time round, accompanied by several excitable friends, we messed around in the snow for days, drinking plenty of local wine and enjoying more than one display of public nudity.

On the face of it, this storyboard offered a bitter-sweet glimpse of lost love and new romance against the backdrop of an opulent Christmas house party, but behind the scenes it became a riotous affair. The fact that our friends were there as extras in the video to a sure-fire Christmas hit single seemed to get lost in their excitement about getting a free holiday. There was an expense account to blow and they were determined to make the most of it. In fairness, so were we. When George and I arrived in Saas-Fee a day late, everybody was already well oiled. Our first evening together came to a premature end when, after a group of us jumped naked into the swimming pool, one friend swallowed half a gallon of chlorinated water and projectile vomited into one of the filters.

With us were George's friend Pat Fernandez, Pepsi and Shirlie and a bunch of other long-term chums, including my friend Dave. The over-exuberance of our skinny-dipping disaster extended into our first day of filming. Laid out on the table of the ski-chalet set was a Christmas banquet: roast turkey and all the trimmings lit by candles and fairy lights. But when our assistant director walked in his face dropped.

'What wally thought *that* would be a good idea?' he asked, pointing to the wine glasses that had been inelegantly filled to the brim. It hardly suggested the level of sophistication required of our 'Last Christmas' party.

'Not to worry, chief,' said Dave as he pushed past the cast and crew. *'I'll see to that for you.'*

In a leisurely but thorough fashion, Dave made his way around the table, adjusting all sixteen glasses, and in the process guzzling the equivalent of at least two bottles of wine. By the time his selfless task was complete, Dave was clearly struggling to stay upright. By the time we wrapped, we were all in the same boat. While there was a seemingly bottomless vat of wine in play, we were forbidden from touching the feast in front of us. And so, in the interests of continuity, we all drank on empty stomachs and got more and more rowdy. Eventually, after crying with laughter had made my eyes puffy and bloodshot, the unimpressed director had to excuse me from the final shot of the dinner scene. I was a mess.

Discipline didn't improve much the next morning when we started filming outside. The script required us to have a snowball fight. Manfully ignoring our hangovers, we gave it our all until, in a scene that would feature prominently in the final cut, I was tossed over a fence and landed so badly I genuinely thought I'd broken something. It would have taken a neck brace for George to notice, though. During breaks in filming he was often found next to the director's chair, looking over the rushes in forensic detail, scrubbing any footage that he felt made him look scruffy, or podgy. Shots in which his hair seemed ever so slightly out of place were also dispatched to the cutting-room floor. On one occasion he became so fixated on his appearance that, after rolling around in the snow with his fictional girlfriend, George insisted on running the film backwards in search of a shot in which he was pouting broodily, rather than a take where he had been laughing and joking that seemed to better suit the scene. In doing so, he unwittingly composed a shot that gives the impression he'd just taken a snowball to the knackers.

The evening concluded with a drunken steeplechase around the hotel balconies. Naked, save for a pair of snow boots, we hurdled the partition walls. The freezing cold ensured that it was a less than impressive sight. After landing breathlessly at the finishing line I turned round to see the director and his wife, quite reasonably thinking they were safe from prying eyes, enjoying some fun of their own. His wife shrieked at the sight of our bums pressed up against the glass as we looked over our shoulders and waved. If our behaviour over the course of the shoot had given him good reason to want to see the back of us, I doubt that this was quite what he had in mind . . .

19. Feeding the World

The invitation to appear on one of the biggest singles in pop history arrived shortly after we returned from Saas-Fee. A fax appeared, requesting my presence at SARM West Studios in Notting Hill on 25 November to contribute to a Christmas single. Beyond that, there was very little other detail, although I knew that SARM was owned by Frankie Goes To Hollywood's producer, Trevor Horn.

I'd been up to my neck in rehearsals for our forthcoming tour. Like so many of the approaches that came in to our management company, I dismissed the fax as being of little importance. That there were no record company names and contact details on it, or travel information, only compounded the impression that it wasn't official business. Only later did I appreciate that the lack of detail was a deliberate effort to keep one of the most momentous recordings in British pop history under wraps until it could be announced to maximum effect. And so I missed out on Band Aid.

While George was in West London, recording 'Do They Know It's Christmas?' with the cream of British rock and pop talent, I was enjoying a lie-in followed by a leisurely Sunday morning with the papers and a bacon and egg sandwich. It was only when I later met up with George for more rehearsals that I finally grasped the magnitude of what had taken place.

Pulled together by Boomtown Rats frontman Bob Geldof and Midge Ure from Ultravox, Band Aid's ranks included members of U2, Heaven 17, Kool & the Gang, Spandau Ballet, Culture Club, Bananarama and Status Quo. Phil Collins, Paul Young and Sting were there too. George should have been happy to be singing alongside them, but he was upset following the recording. Paul Weller had taken exception to George's description earlier in the year of miners' union leader Arthur Scargill as 'a wanker' and told him so. Unknowingly Weller had hit a raw nerve.

Wham! had been a controversial addition to the bill at a miners' strike benefit gig at the Royal Festival Hall a few months previously. 'Club Tropicana' had been seen by the music press as a betrayal of the social conscience in evidence on 'Wham Rap' and 'Young Guns'. Our decision to appear at the benefit dressed all in white didn't help lend us political gravitas either. We then annoyed the organisers when George insisted we lip-sync our set rather than play the songs live. He hated not being in complete control of our sound and, given some of the snide comments over our inclusion, was paranoid that one of the sound engineers might attempt to nobble us. We were conscious of a growing antipathy towards Wham! from music snobs within the industry and George believed we were being undermined at every opportunity. He didn't want our detractors to land another cheap shot.

'But we're good enough,' I reasoned beforehand. 'We play live all the time. It's going to be fine.'

George shook his head. 'No, we'll have a backing tape. That way no one can mess with us.'

I tried to argue that lip-syncing might prove counter-productive. I feared it would hand our detractors even more ammunition to aim at us if word were to leak out, only reinforcing a view within music circles that Wham! was not the Real Deal.

It wasn't the first time either. There had been similar trouble when we had played on Channel 4's *The Tube*. It prided itself on being a live show, but once again George antagonised everybody by insisting we lip-sync as if we were on *Top of the Pops*. His need to have complete control over our sound meant he would not be persuaded, but his inflexibility backfired horribly. After we'd performed the first of two songs, the sound engineer started the second track while George was still introducing it. He was incandescent. As far as he was concerned, our performance had been maliciously scuppered on live TV, making us a laughing stock.

Well, you bloody asked for that, mate, I thought. It had been a pratfall entirely of his own making.

But to then be confronted by Paul Weller during the recording of 'Do They Know It's Christmas?' – *a charity event* – only amplified George's feeling that he was under siege. He felt Weller's comments were inappropriate, but, most importantly, it wasn't how he would have treated another artist in a similar position. George was at Band Aid because it was an altruistic gesture he wanted to support. To then be grilled by another artist in the same position was distressing.

While I was able to shrug off any criticism of me for not attending the recording, it hardly meant that I was unmoved by the situation in Ethiopia. The reporting of the famine from the BBC's Michael Buerk was horrific and incredibly disturbing and, as we looked forward to the release of 'Last Christmas', George and I decided to donate our royalties from its release to the same cause. It seemed only right to try to do whatever we could to help. And, now that we were free of the Innervision deal, that help had the potential to be substantial.

Both 'Last Christmas' and 'Do They Know It's Christmas?' were being released on the same day. We had become very competitive about Wham!'s chart performance but on this occasion we were just going to have to accept that our song, which had felt like a number 1 record from the day George had first sketched it out, was going to be kept off the top spot, and that was as it should be.

'Do They Know It's Christmas?' launched like a rocket, selling a million copies in its first week to become the fastest-selling single of all time, then quickly shifting another three million more to become the then biggest-ever UK single. 'Last Christmas', backed by the B-side, 'Everything She Wants', remained at number 2 in the charts for thirteen weeks. We had achieved the 'Trivial Pursuit answer' honour of releasing the biggest-selling single not to get to number 1.

I'd be lying if I said that George and I weren't a little conflicted about it. Of course we were delighted that Band Aid raised so much money for Ethiopian famine relief, but there was, at the same time, an undertow of disappointment. It was easier for me to reconcile my feelings about the situation, especially as the success of both singles was contributing to the same vital cause, but it was different for George. Chart success was an important affirmation of his self-worth and getting to number 1 had really mattered to him. We were soon making jokes about the perennial bridesmaid status of 'Last Christmas', but underneath the gags I knew he was smarting a little.

Happily, a few months later, there was validation of his talent from another source. The prestigious Ivor Novello Awards recognised songwriters and by 1985 Wham! had established enough of a presence to receive nominations in three separate categories. It was an emotional event for both of us. At first there was further disappointment when 'Wake Me Up Before You Go-Go' missed out in the Best Song category to Phil Collins's 'Against All Odds'. But 'Careless Whisper' then won the award for Most Performed Work – or, in other words, the Song Most Played on the Radio. It was a flattering recognition of the song's broad appeal, but there was a bigger prize at stake. George was in line for the Songwriter of the Year award and, as the nominees were read out, my mind was set. I had decided that if George didn't win, I was going to return our Most Performed Work award in protest. There was no doubt in my mind that George deserved it more than any of his rivals.

When he was eventually announced as that year's winner, it was an incredibly moving moment. The Ivor Novellos were the only music-industry awards that really seemed to matter to George at that time because they were decided by an academy of songwriters, composers and authors – his peers – rather than critics or record company executives. They carried a credibility and weight that George valued and respected. After accepting his award from one of his own heroes, Elton John, George was quite overcome. He found it impossible to hold back the tears during his acceptance speech. Watching him from the audience, it was hard not to follow suit. He'd been embraced by the people he most admired and identified with. The whole world would be next.

DAILY
EXPRESS
THE VOICE OF BRITAIN

Thursday March 14 1985 ● 20p ● TV Pages 20 and 21

Tears as George receives his trophy Picture: DOUGLAS MORRISON

Andrew comforts his partner

Weep year
for Wham!

POP STAR George Michael of Wham wept on stage yesterday when he was named Songwriter of the Year at the Ivor Novello Awards in London.

The 21-year-old heartthrob broke down after receiving the trophy from Elton John. He said: "This is the most important thing that has ever happened to me."

George and Wham partner Andrew Ridgeley also won the Most Performed Work award for their hit song Careless Whisper.

20. The Clothes Show

At the end of 1984, *Make It Big* was still riding high in the UK charts and around the world. Most encouraging was the fact that Whamania was taking off in America where, after reaching number 1 in the *Billboard* charts, the album was well on its way to selling an incredible six million copies. On top of the success of *Make It Big*, I was excited about touring again, especially as, after the craziness of the Club Fantastic tour, we'd be doing so in some style. Cramped tour buses and poky hotel rooms were a thing of the past. We were also looking beyond the UK this time. As far as we were concerned, America and the Far East were the Next Frontiers for any self-respecting pop band. But we started the Big Tour in the slightly less exotic surroundings of Whitley Bay Ice Rink before a brief whizz around the UK throughout December, including dates on Christmas Eve and Boxing Day at Wembley Arena. Only then did we fly to Japan to begin our next big adventure.

Japan was the Premier League. An extraordinary collision of East and West, ancient and modern, where bands were greeted with the kind of hysteria associated with Beatlemania.

Judging by the screams that greeted us on our arrival, we were as popular in Japan as we were at home. And then some. Of our contemporaries perhaps only Duran Duran enjoyed a similar reception. Wham! merchandise was thrust in front of our faces at every turn, along with a relentless demand for autographs. The rapture that surrounded us seemed almost religious in its fervour. And at the centre of it all, two kids from Hertfordshire sporting bouffant hair and baggy tartan suits. It was surreal.

The tartan represented something of a sartorial upgrade from skimpy Fila shorts. Wham! had never really pushed the boat out in terms of fashion. In an era where the likes of David Bowie, Adam Ant and Culture Club were expressing themselves with extravagant tailoring and wild haircuts, George and I had struggled to compete. Cash-strapped, we'd relied on Levi's jeans and high street fashion, not Galliano, Alexander McQueen, Issey Miyake and Comme des Garçons.

Not any more.

With royalties beginning to trickle in from our new record deal, I was now able to mix in a few select pieces from high-end designers. I didn't go crazy. The big money and the Ferrari were still a little way off,

WHAM JAPAN TOUR '85

DATE	VENUE	TRAVEL	HOTEL
Jan 7 MON		1:30pm Baggage Down 2:30pm Depart Hotel 2:40pm Lv TOKYO by ANA#259 5:25pm Arr FUKUOKA	MIYAKO HOTEL TOKYO 1-1-50, Shirogane-dai Minato-ku, Tokyo PH: 03-447-3111 TLX: 242-3111
Jan 8 TUE	FUKUOKA SUN PALACE 092-272-1123 8:00am Stage call 4:00pm Sound check 6:00pm Doors open 6:30pm SHOW Time	7:30am Crew Depart 3:30pm Band Depart	ZENNIKU HOTEL (ANA) 3-3-3, Hakata Ekimae PH: 092-471-7111
Jan 9 WED	OFF	1:00pm Baggage Down 1:45pm Depart Hotel 2:50pm Lv FUKUOKA by ANA#210 3:50pm Arr OSAKA	HOTEL NIKKO (JAL) OSAKA
Jan 10 THU	OSAKA FESTIVAL HALL PH: 06-231-2221 9:00am Stage call 4:00pm Sound check 5:45pm Doors open 6:30pm Show time	3:30pm Band Depart	HOTEL NIKKO (JAL) OSAKA 7, Nishino-cho Minami-ku, Osaka PH: 06-244-1111 TLX: 522-7575
Jan 11 FRI	OSAKA TAIIKUKAN PH: 06-631-0121 8:00am Stage call 4:00pm Sound check 5:30pm Doors Open 6:30pm show time	7:20am Crew depart 3:30pm Band depart 10:30pm Baggage down	Ditto

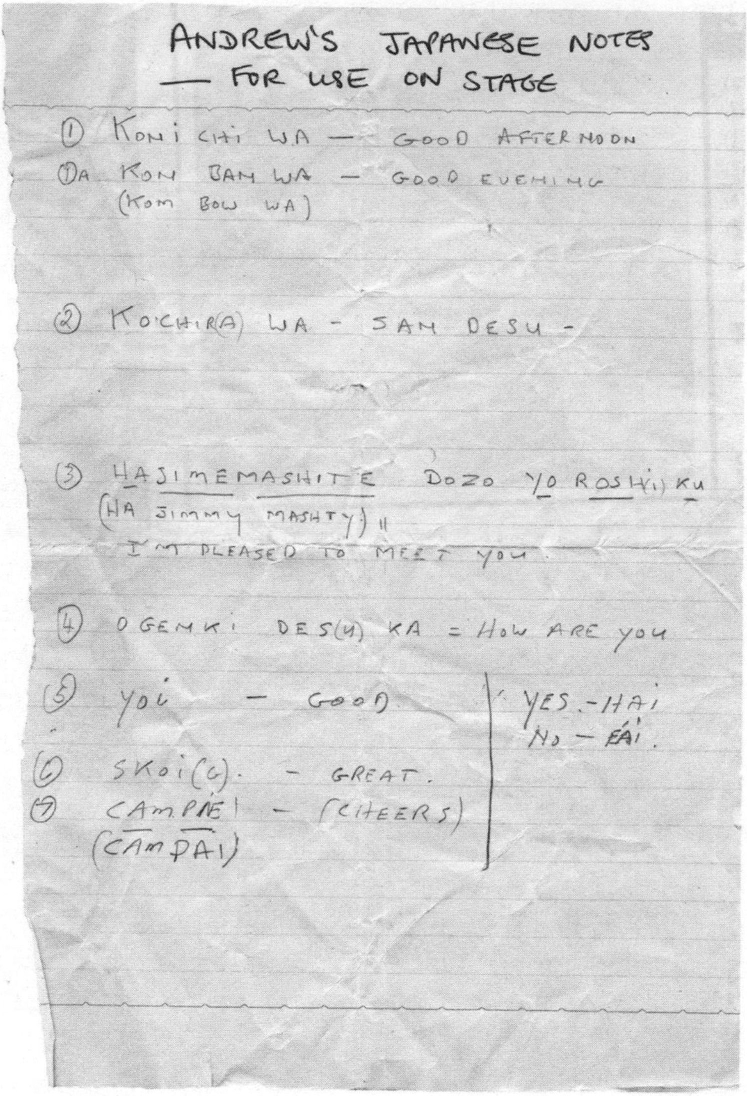

ANDREW'S JAPANESE NOTES
— FOR USE ON STAGE

① KONICHI WA — GOOD AFTERNOON
①A KON BAM WA — GOOD EVENING
(KOM BOW WA)

② KOCHIRA) WA - SAM DESU -

③ HAJIMEMASHITE DOZO YO ROSHI KU
(HA JIMMY MASHTY) ‖
I'M PLEASED TO MEET YOU.

④ O GEMKI DES(U) KA = HOW ARE YOU

⑤ YOI — GOOD | YES. – HAI
                       | NO — EAI.

⑥ SKOI(G). — GREAT.
⑦ CAMPIE! — (CHEERS)
(CAMPAI)

but I was excited to finally be in a position where I could treat myself to stylish clothes. And the options now available to me had increased dramatically. They weren't just nice to have, but a necessity. It was imperative to look different in every photo shoot and there were so many going on that the choice of clothes had to keep up. While there was nobody actually telling me and George what to wear, we sometimes used stylists who would show up with a rack of different clothes for us to try out. A lot of the time, the clothes that were brought to us were too garish or over the top – it was the mid eighties after all – and neither of us looked to the catwalk for sartorial inspiration. Fashion per se wasn't my thing, but looking good was and the two didn't necessarily go hand in hand. I had always had a sense of style that was very much my own and as Wham! became bigger, I gravitated towards my own aesthetic tastes rather than the styling adopted by many other bands. That no longer included the kilt I'd inflicted on the Executive's audience, but jackets and suits. It was 1984, though, and so some of the designers I went for still liked to err on the side of flamboyance.

While I rarely identified with one particular artist or style icon, I'd long admired the blueprint laid down by the likes of Bowie and later Bryan Ferry, who often offset a very sharp suit with an unbuttoned shirt and floppy fringe. I bought coats from Yohji and Versace and tried to combine contemporary trends with the

restrained elegance displayed by Ferry. But only off duty. Onstage I needed something more eye-catching. I wanted to bring a little more flair to the party. I wanted outfits that meant I could be picked out at a distance and that were, of necessity, distinct from George's. The latter was straightforward enough given that George had decided on a look that defied all rational discourse.

I don't think that George had an instinct for fashion. There were blouses and frilly shirts. Baggy, John Craven-style knitwear and clumpy boots featured heavily too. Sometimes I wished that George would nudge me and ask for an opinion before he dressed for a show or personal appearance, because his outfits could sometimes look a little strange. Yet one of the few things George rarely consulted me on were his stylistic choices. If he had, I might have counselled against the bolero jacket and tight leggings, royal-blue silk cummerbund and Chinese slippers. It was an ensemble that seemed to have been inspired by Rudolf Nureyev.

At least George's self-consciousness and concern about his weight seemed to be diminishing. There remained, though, a constant struggle with his hair. Concern in the eighties about the expanding hole in the ozone layer might have been connected with his insatiable appetite for hairspray. George bleached, teased and blow-dried to such an extent that friends who caught a glimpse of him on the front page of tabloids sometimes mistook him for Princess Diana.

When I was asked in an interview what annoyed me most about touring with my old schoolmate, I complained, 'The burning smell, the faffing about with his hairdryer, the fiddling around is endless . . .'

By contrast, I was feeling pretty pleased with my

get-up. Accessorised with a dangly Wild West-style bow tie, I wore a full-length Royal Stewart tartan coat with white 'art' silk lining and metal chain fastenings. I completed the outfit with a matching tailored jacket and slim-fitting trousers and a white shirt. And I thought it all looked rather eye-catching and just the ticket for the job in hand.

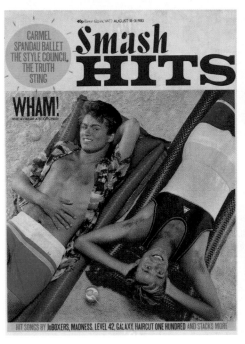

Above: Meeting Her Maj at a polo event in Windsor, introduced by the late, much-missed Bryan Morrison. The Queen was extremely nice to us (I doubt she had a clue to whom she'd been introduced) and engaged us in conversation about our recent visit to China.

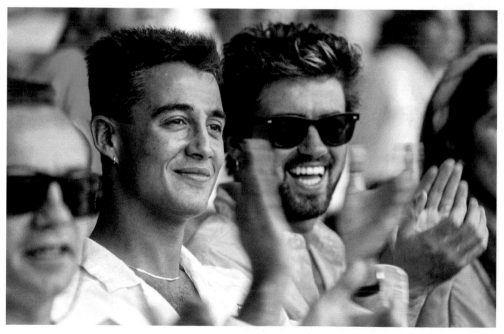

Above: Live Aid. There was a lot to applaud that day!

Above: Elton on stage for the encores at The Final. One of his more bizarre get ups!

Above: ANDY, ANDY, ANDY, ANDY, ANDY, ANDY, ANDY, ANDY, George, ANDY, ANDY . . .

WHAM! The Final, Saturday 28 June 1986. Not a bad way to bring the curtain down!

Above: Rock in Rio, 1991. And I thought Wembley was a big crowd!

Below: With Pepsi and Shirlie, giving our tribute to George. I felt it was especially important that we gave voice to the public's grief; there had been no real occasion where it might have been expressed until that point.

21. Orient Excess

'How do you feel about playing in China?'

When Simon and Jazz first mooted the idea of travelling to what was then considered an unfriendly communist state, neither George nor I were too taken by it. We had barely made our first steps into America, after playing just six theatre shows, so performing in somewhere as off the wall as China felt genuinely crackers, but there was method behind the madness. Simon understood the power of a grand attention-grabbing gesture, and he also knew that George's reluctance to embark on an extensive tour of the States was going to severely impair our ability to break the US market big time and capitalise on the success of *Make It Big*. Denied the exposure that a major nationwide tour, with all its attendant local publicity, would generate, Simon knew he had to come up with something that would give us more bang for our buck. He needed to create a little hype. And in his own inimitable way, Simon came to the conclusion that the best way to do that was to

introduce Wham!'s effervescent brand of pop to the Middle Kingdom. By becoming the first Western band to perform there, we would garner headlines in America and around the world. Or so went the theory.

I still felt China was a crackpot idea! I knew the trip was going to cost us a fortune and I wasn't entirely convinced that the two gigs being arranged by Simon in Peking and Canton (this was long before Westerners took to calling them Beijing and Guangzhou) would actually attract the global attention he thought it would. China was so far off the radar that Simon's plan seemed to be based on faith more than evidence. It was hit and hope.

But Simon remained convinced and had been

shuttling to and from China as we'd recorded *Make It Big*, striking all sorts of deals with various political figures to ensure our performances could go ahead. Once he had played his trump card and explained to George that his master plan would spare us from the need to crisscross America touring and fulfilling endless radio and TV promo obligations, we agreed to go along with it. Simon's scheme also made a similarly gruelling European tour surplus to requirements. Instead, we were going to strike out into uncharted territory.

Wham! was about to make pop history.

We flew into Peking in April 1985. In real life, the country seemed to exist just as it had in my imagination.

269

Streets echoed with the sound of tinkling bells as hundreds and hundreds of cyclists whizzed along. Nearly all of them were dressed in the drab Mao suit of grey tunic and matching trousers. It was supposed to be a symbol of Chinese unity, but I don't think they had too much choice in the matter. Meanwhile, only one Western-style hotel existed in the city and so we were installed there. Although comparatively modern, its fixtures and fittings were basic compared to what we had become used to at home and abroad. For some reason everything smelled of chemicals. But it was people's reaction to us that struck me most. It's easy to forget now just how closed and insular China was at the time. Everyone we encountered seemed to be wary of us.

We soon came to feel a bit trapped by it. We were set to stay in China for ten days but had been prohibited from exploring the city away from the official tours being arranged for us. Minders followed us everywhere. We travelled to the Great Wall of China and visited temples; we were escorted to a local food market as part of a cultural excursion where we played 'Wake Me Up Before You Go-Go' on a tape deck to a crowd of bemused local workers, most of them in their sixties and seventies. At grand banquets we even ate wildly exotic meats and vegetables, most of them unfamiliar to us. And an atmosphere of cautious curiosity trailed us everywhere we went. It was all very different to the screaming girls and autograph-chasers that mobbed

us everywhere else. Instead I shook hands with government ministers and bowed my head deferentially to China's great and good. In one surreal episode, I found myself addressing a room full of dignitaries at a fancy dinner in an ornate city hall. I did my best to establish some kind of connection.

'My partner George and I both feel that the nature of our performance is in many ways similar to some facets of Chinese theatre,' I said. The two of us had been bickering about the speech only moments earlier, both unsure of what tone to strike in a culture that was entirely alien to us. I wasn't even sure if opening with 'Ladies and gentlemen . . .' would be appropriate. Were there going to be any women in attendance? I didn't

GOOD NEWS!
EXTRA SEATS ADDED AGAIN

JESU INTERNATIONAL ENTERTAINMENT LTD. proudly presents

WHAM!
HK'85

Book Now

HIT SONGS INCLUDE:
CARELESS WHISPER | FREEDOM
WAKE ME UP BEFORE YOU GO GO

APRIL 2nd, 3rd, '85 (8pm)
PLACE : HONG KONG COLISEUM
TICKET PRICE : $120, & $80
AVAILABLE AT : TOM LEE PIANO CO. BRANCHES
Man Yee Bldg. Cameron Lane)
CENTURY CINEMA

know. But whatever we did, and wherever we went, there was the constant sense our actions were being scrutinised, the Chinese authorities fearing their youth might be overly influenced by two Western pop stars with flamboyant hairstyles and a wardrobe of Phillips Tailor's tartan suits. We were only playing China in the hope it might save us from touring America. The Chinese Communist Party, meanwhile, appeared to be unsure about the wisdom of having agreed to our visit. There was an unusual strain to everything we did.

This awkwardness was never more evident than when we played our first gig at the People's Gymnasium in Peking, a vast indoor space capable of seating fifteen thousand people. It had previously been best known outside China for hosting the World Table Tennis Championships in 1961. Before we walked onstage, ticket holders were warned not to celebrate our arrival too exuberantly and I later heard that leaflets had been issued to fans before the show carrying strict instructions about how to behave. The Minister of Culture was even encouraging Chinese kids to 'watch, but not learn' from our performance. After taking to the stage I noticed lines of police officers, all facing the audience in an intimidating wall of authority. Each new Wham! fan had been a given free cassette of our songs with their ticket. On one side our songs appeared in their original form. On the reverse our opening act, a local Chinese singer called Cheng Fangyuan, had covered tracks like 'Club Tropicana' and 'Wake Me Up Before You Go-Go' in Chinese. The lyrics had been rewritten with a distinctively communist flavour.

> Wake me up before you go-go,
> Compete with the sky to go high-high.
> Wake me up before you go-go,
> Men fight to be first to reach the peak.
> Wake me up before you go-go,
> Women are on the same journey and will not
>   fall behind.

Quite. I couldn't have put it better myself.

As we started to play, it was impossible not to feel similarly off kilter. Christ, this isn't going to be the usual show . . . I thought as the synth pop of 'Bad Boys' played incongruously over the heads of hundreds of stiff-backed cops, all facing away from the stage. There were small pockets of dancing. Foreign students, lucky not to live under the same restrictive rules as everyone else in the vast room, were allowed to enjoy themselves, but when one local man joined in the fun, several officers descended upon him and warned him to stay in his seat. When he then kicked up a fuss, he was forcefully dragged away. Pepsi and Shirlie were both really upset by the incident and it was hard not to imagine that he had been given a terrible beating or, worse, sentenced to a period of hard labour at some god-awful detention camp. But despite the uneasy atmosphere, the gig would prove to be something of a watershed. Years later, once China had become a more open and welcoming state, stories about the impact we'd made on China's younger generations began to emerge. Kids had apparently sought out jeans and denim jackets. Others tried to track down more Western music, which opened the doors for other British and American bands to perform there, with the Police following in our footfalls shortly afterwards.

While I was intrigued by the gulf between life in China and my own existence in a Western liberal democracy, George could not have given two hoots. He was concerned solely with the music. Despite the eye-opening strangeness on display beyond our touring bubble, he remained cocooned inside, preoccupied with the latest international and album charts and, in particular, news of *Make It Big*'s latest sales. He'd become obsessed with the numbers. It was his only real measure of success and so functioned as a barometer of how he was growing as a songwriter. By comparison, reviews and column inches meant little to him. In China, he only left his hotel room for shows, or the next VIP meet-and-greet on the itinerary. And when he did, trailed by a gaggle of Western photographers and journalists, he took very little interest in the local culture, architecture or landscape around us. The physical experience of travelling just didn't appeal to him. Music was so all-consuming that he rarely considered anything else. It bordered on pathological, and our radio plugger, Gary Farrow, was hounded by George for the latest mid-week chart positions, radio plays and sales numbers. Hits indicated that his songwriting was good. Number 1s meant it was the best. As far as George was concerned, our Chinese adventure could only be considered worthwhile if it fuelled global record sales.

In an effort to squeeze greater exposure from our trip, Simon felt we should document it on film. Then he chose director Lindsay Anderson, who was famous for bleak social realist films like *This Sporting Life* and *Look Back In Anger*. While the value of capturing everything on film was obvious enough, the choice of Anderson as director seemed absolutely bonkers. Simon had liked the idea of using him because his involvement lent the project gravitas and artistic credibility, while George was all for it simply because he admired Anderson's political and social outlook, but neither made him the right choice. But although I struggled to see the point of having someone seemingly so totally at odds with the idea of a Wham! publicity stunt, I played along whenever the cameras were pointed at me. If I'm honest I wasn't sure anything was going to come of it all.

It would not be through any lack of material, though. If our second show was anything to go by, Whamania seemed to be trying to find expression. In Canton, there was far more raucous energy in evidence and fans were even allowed to dance in their seats. Then the

DAILY EXPRESS Monday April 1 1985

THERE'S SO MUCH M—

China bound Wham! make it a family affair

By DAVID WIGG

TOP pop duo Wham! lined their parents up for a very special treat yesterday.

As the smash-hit singing pair left Britain on the first leg of their trip to China, both sets of parents went too —a thank-you present for all their help and support.

In all there were 96 people, including minders, sound engineers and film crew, on board the group's Hong Kong-bound plane.

Star George Michael, pictured with his parents

Jack and Lesley Pales (above, left) said : " I like my parents travelling with me. I feel I owe them that.

"The closeness we have as a family has prevented me from ever feeling lonely in spite of the pressures of this business," he added.

Andrew Ridgeley was just as keen to have his parents Albert and Jenny (right) along too.

After playing two concerts

in Hong Kong, the entourage will move on for the first visit of a Western group to Communist China.

A lavish banquet in their honour is to be held in Peking on Friday night.

The historic tour is being filmed by top British director Lindsay Anderson.

George, 21, enthused : " We need to have it caught on celluloid because we can hardly believe it's happening. We are overjoyed about being allowed into China. It's a fantastic coup."

George always wore a tea cosy on his head for long-haul flights.

sax introduction to 'Careless Whisper' triggered an outbreak of actual screaming! But perhaps the most memorable image of the trip ended up being a much more affecting one. The sight of me and George posing on the Great Wall of China with a three- or four-year-old boy dressed in a military uniform, an officer's cap perched on his head, appeared to sum up the gulf between us. And it was this cultural divide that seemed to capture the imagination of the world's media. It may not have had an immediate effect on record sales, but it made Wham! feel like a global cultural phenomenon.

I returned home grateful for the liberties that allowed us the freedom to express ourselves. China had been like visiting the moon.

Sadly, Lindsay Anderson's film failed to capture it all in anything like the way we had hoped. George and I arrived typically late to an intimate screening of the film, now titled *If You Were There*. We needn't have bothered. The film was exactly what I'd feared: a well-shot but drearily worthy look at life in a communist state, rather than the exciting adventures of a Western pop band in China. George was unimpressed, as was I, and, for now at least, the film was junked as a project in need of dramatic remedial work. The tone and style of the movie displayed so little understanding of what was required that, if it was ever going to see the light of day, it would effectively have to be remade, salvaging whatever we could from the original material.

It was a real missed opportunity, but not quite the final sting in the tail our trip to China had to offer. There was also the bill. We had paid for everything only to discover that any money we'd made would be staying in China because the authorities would not sanction cash transactions to non-nationals. A shipment of several hundred worker's bicycles was offered in lieu of cash, but we politely declined.

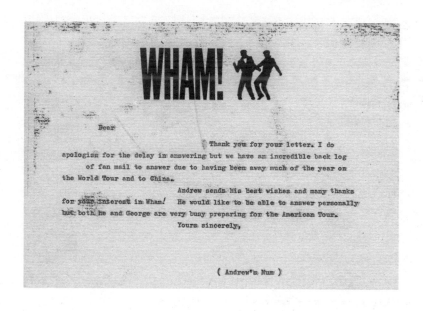

22. Come Together

George's singing had the power to raise the hairs on the back of my neck. I'd first got a sense of that when he wrote and recorded 'Wake Me Up Before You Go-Go', but with the Big Tour, George's development as a singer and songwriter seemed to be accelerating. It all seemed to reflect a growing self-confidence in him. He wasn't yet the finished article, but people were beginning to realise that he was the real deal. No more so than in America.

When Wham! had first travelled to the States, appearing on TV programmes like *American Bandstand* and *Solid Gold*, US fans and critics got us immediately. We were embraced as a pure pop band without any of the complications the more socially aware lyrics of 'Wham Rap' and 'Young Guns' had caused us in the UK. And, especially after the number 1 success of 'Careless Whisper' in the States, George had been identified as a songwriter on the rise.

Such was his growing reputation that he was invited

to perform at the Apollo Theatre's fiftieth birthday cel-
ebrations in Harlem, New York. The legendary venue
became renowned for hosting shows by incredible artists such as Aretha Franklin, Otis Redding, Marvin
Gaye and James Brown, who recorded a number of live
albums there. The list of singers taking part in the gala
show reads like a *Who's Who*: Stevie Wonder, Diana

Ross, Little Richard, Al Green, Joe Cocker, Rod Stewart and many more were invited to perform during a six-hour show, with proceeds from the event going to the Ethiopian famine relief project. Also on the bill, despite his relatively young age of twenty-one, was George, who performed duets with Smokey Robinson and Stevie Wonder. I don't think he'd ever sung with anybody of the stature of either of those two before. But as I watched from the balcony, surrounded by an A-list crowd, George performed flawlessly, lacing Stevie Wonder's classic 'Love's In Need Of Love Today' with his own distinctive style and character. As he traded vocal lines with the great man himself, George confirmed my strongly held belief that he was every bit the equal of the people he was sharing the stage with that night.

He was fantastic. So good in fact that at times it even surprised me. His rendition of 'Careless Whisper' with Smokey Robinson sounded incredible. Suddenly it felt as if I wasn't the only one who truly understood the scale of George's talent. Everybody could see it, and once again I was reminded that George's ultimate destination lay beyond Wham!. He was finally touching the heights he had always been capable of. Outside of Wham!, the only constraints on George would be the ones set by himself. As the crowd rose to their feet for a standing ovation following his epic, gospel-infused duet with Stevie Wonder, there was little doubt that we were in the presence of greatness.

END OF THE BIG TOUR PARTY
Sunday 3rd March
You and one guest are invited
to help participate in the
festivities to end three months
of hard graft around the world.
at
Legends, 29 Old Burlington Street, London W1.
Admittance by invitation only - don't leave it at home.

Dress: Decently

from
9.30 pm onwards

George had taken a huge leap forward. But it was just the beginning.

Two months later, on 13 July 1985, George was back in London to perform on his biggest stage to date. And Wembley Stadium was packed to the rafters for Live Aid. After the runaway success of Band Aid, Bob Geldof and Midge Ure had harnessed all the goodwill and momentum and turned it into the biggest charity gig of all time. Across the Atlantic in Philadelphia, another stadium was also full to capacity.

I felt exhausted just imagining the effort it must have taken to draw up the day's extraordinary line-up of the

greatest names in pop and rock history. In London, the bill included the Boomtown Rats, Spandau Ballet, Nik Kershaw, Sting, U2, Dire Straits, Queen, David Bowie, The Who, Elton John and Paul McCartney. In Philadelphia, the roll call was no less impressive. The audience in the JFK Stadium could look forward to acts like the Four Tops, Black Sabbath, Run-DMC, Madonna, Bryan Adams, Simple Minds, the Beach Boys, Tina Turner, Tom Petty, Neil Young, Eric Clapton, Bob Dylan and various Rolling Stones.

But perhaps the biggest coup on the American bill was a performance from a specially re-formed Led Zeppelin. Led Zep had disbanded in 1980 following the death of their original drummer, John Bonham, and had drafted in Phil Collins for their return.

I'd been a big fan since school, after George had been given their entire back catalogue by a family friend. And playing a bit myself, I was in awe of guitarist Jimmy Page's wonderful musicianship and sound. To my amazement, I'd actually met Page in the flesh the previous year during The Big Tour. While I was waiting backstage, there had been a knock on my dressing-room door. It was our Tour Director, Ken Watts, who appeared a little flustered.

'Er, Andrew,' he said. 'I've got a bit of a weird one for you. Jimmy Page is here with his daughter and was wondering if you could come out to say hello.'

My head span. *Jimmy Page was waiting to meet me.* The

finer details of who he was with and what on earth he might be doing here evaporated in an instant. I couldn't hear, I couldn't think, completely discombobulated by the idea that one of the most iconic musicians in rock'n'roll history, a guitar god, was just outside the door. I composed myself, stepped outside and came face-to-face with Jimmy, who was standing patiently with his young daughter. It really was him – this was not a wind-up.

Bloody hell. Bloody hell. Bloody hell . . . I thought. That is Jimmy Page.

And then an awful realisation struck me. *Oh, my God, I can't believe he's been dragged to a bloody Wham! concert. Surely the last thing he wants to go to is a bloody Wham!*

concert . . . ? But there was no turning back. I shook his hand and grinned like an idiot.

'My daughter's a really big fan,' he said, smiling back. 'It's so good of you to meet with us.'

I felt as though I'd stepped into an alternative reality. Here I was, a twenty-one-year-old kid, a member of a band synonymous with breezy pop hooks and club-friendly dance routines, being treated with deferential courtesy by one of the most revered rock guitarists of all time. I felt totally knocked off stride. After enduring ninety minutes of Wham! live, I suspected the high priest of hell-scorched blues probably felt the same way. At least, with Led Zep performing in the Philadelphia half of the show, there would be no repeat of that at Live Aid. But the feelings that accompanied my arrival at Wembley with George weren't entirely dissimilar. In appearing at Wembley Stadium I would be fulfilling something of a childhood dream and yet I couldn't help feeling a little embarrassed. Next to names like Queen, Paul McCartney or the Who, we were new kids on the block and barely out of nappies. It seemed utterly perverse that we would be sharing the same global stage as acts of that stature. And compounding the feeling of dislocation was the fact that I wasn't even really performing at Live Aid. Not officially.

George had been invited to perform 'Don't Let The Sun Go Down On Me' with Elton John. I would just be joining them onstage to help out on the backing vocals. As a result I spent much of the day feeling like a spare part. At the same time, though, I was aware of how valuable we were to the cause. The aim of the event was to raise as much money as possible for Ethiopian famine relief and Bob and Midge knew that a broad range of acts from different genres would maximise international awareness, interest and donations. Wham! was now such a massive deal that our involvement, along with that of bands like Duran Duran, helped ensure Live Aid's appeal to younger generations of fans. George and I were determined to do whatever we could to help.

Bob Geldof buzzed around backstage greeting old friends and introducing himself to anyone he hadn't met before. It was evident to us all that he was an unstoppable force, bulldozing even the most stubborn personalities into submission. There was no way he was going to let any A-lister distract him from the job at hand. All the same, while he was jabbing his finger and demanding 'Give us yer bloody money' of the public, he was a little more soothing and polite when he approached me and George. The effect was the same, though.

'Cheers for coming, you two,' he greeted us, before immediately pressing me into action. 'You know, it would be great if you could go upstairs and do your bit, Andrew. Get on the telly and appeal to the Great British Public for some money.' I didn't hesitate. Not that I ever had any choice in the matter! He was irresistible. He'd driven everything forward with such a relentless, tireless energy that it was impossible not to be overwhelmed by the physical, emotional and organisational effort involved.

As we looked forward to taking to the stage after dark, the day passed in an exhilarating, awe-inspiring blur. My TV appeal was actually a brief respite from the sensory overload going on all around. Wherever you turned there seemed to be another legendary figure that we'd previously admired from afar: Bowie, Freddie Mercury, Bryan Ferry.

George was confident that when it came to his performance he would rise to the occasion. But while he was thrilled and honoured that he'd be singing with Elton, he was some way from accepting that he now belonged in the same orbit as someone like him. On the back of things like the Ivor Novello Award and Apollo Theatre performance, he was getting there, but he still regarded these music industry greats as heroes rather than peers. He was aware, though, his Live Aid performance had the potential to surprise a few people. And it was being broadcast live around the world to an audience of billions. Compared to some of the other bands on the bill, we knew that Wham! – beyond the teenage audience at least – were considered to be somewhat lightweight. George approached his duet with Elton as a chance to turn some heads with his vocal performance. Raising money was the name of the game, but if anyone listening thought, Crikey, that Wham! bloke really can sing . . . on the back of it, then so much the better. And 'Don't Let The Sun Go Down On Me' was the perfect song with which to do it. It was stitched into George's musical DNA. If he'd been asked to compile a list of 'the tracks that made me' he'd have included it for sure, but it was also perfectly suited to his voice. The stage was set for one of George's most memorable and important performances.

The sight that greeted me as I peered out from backstage with George was extraordinary. An ocean of seventy-two thousand happy people stretched back and up seemingly forever. The atmosphere among them was unique. When the likes of Queen or the Rolling Stones played Wembley there was something congregational about it – a band of worshippers all gathered to see the one band they loved. Today it was about much more than the music. There was an inclusive, communal feel that lent it a very different kind of intensity to any shows I'd been to in the past. And it dawned on me that I'd never appeared in front of an audience that large before. As Elton's duet with Kiki Dee on 'Don't Go Breaking My Heart' drew to a close, the sense of excitement was overwhelming.

   'I'm going to introduce a friend of mine now who's going to sing one of my songs,' Elton began. 'And this guy I admire very much, for his musical talent more than anything else. So, onstage' – ushering George towards his piano – 'Mr George Michael . . . and Mr Andrew Ridgeley.'

The noise on our arrival was deafening, a roar of cheers and screams as George took the microphone and announced that 'Don't Let The Sun Go Down On Me' was one of his favourite Elton John songs. I joined Kiki Dee at the back of the stage as Elton began to play the opening bars of the song. It required a swooping vocal performance, but George was cruising through it in a thrilling display of power. As far as I was concerned George was, alongside Freddie Mercury, one of the two greatest-ever British vocalists. At Live Aid a billion people got to see that for themselves.

George owned the stage.

As the crowd joined in on the chorus, it was as if he was emerging as a different artist before their eyes. The energy around Wembley swept over us. And when Bob and Midge cajoled everyone back onstage for the big finale, a group singalong of 'Do They Know It's Christmas?', the adrenaline was still surging through me. As we walked onstage again, I turned to see that we were being trailed by the likes of David Bowie, Elton, Roger Daltrey, Sting and Mark Knopfler. I looked around, clutching the lyric sheet I'd been given in case I forgot the words. Understandable really, given that I'd managed to miss the song's recording in the first

place. Then suddenly I was sandwiched between Paul McCartney and Bono, and, just as I had the previous year when I met Jimmy Page, I seemed to experience a strange, existential wobble.

'I think you know the next song,' said Bob, ushering in the opening chords of 'Do They Know It's Christmas?' 'It might be a bit of a cock-up, but if you're gonna cock it up you may as well do it with two billion people watching you. So let's cock it up together . . .'

The view ahead was incredible, an endless sea of humanity bouncing up and down in unison, but the view alongside me was just surreal. There was Freddie Mercury, draping his arm around my shoulders as we sang Band Aid's call-and-response chorus together. 'Feed the world! Let them know it's Christmas time . . .' Live Aid had been a party from start to finish; band rivalries and creative differences had been forgotten and egos put aside. It didn't matter about individual performances, or 'cock-ups'. Quite evidently, the people involved understood they were part of something bigger.

That didn't make the fact I was sharing a microphone with Freddie Mercury any easier to comprehend. Queen was part of the soundtrack to my youth and countless after-school listening sessions with George, and all I could think of was how much I wanted to tell him I loved his band's music. (*Freddie, I saw you in '79 at Ally Pally, you were absolutely awesome . . . And actually, I also went to the show at Earls Court . . .*) But the moment never came. I never had another chance to tell him how much Queen had meant to me during my teenage years. As the Live Aid collective were ushered away, Freddie walked stage left, disappearing from view.

And I knew that, for me at least, George would soon be doing the same.

23. The End of a Party

George's star turn at Live Aid, coming on top of success at a handful of US gigs during the Big Tour, gave us the confidence to plan a series of stadium shows. Through August and September, the Whamamerica! tour would take in stadiums in Illinois, Toronto, LA, Oakland, Houston, Miami, Philadelphia and Pontiac. *Make It Big* was a multi-platinum success by that time and we were determined to play in venues that could accommodate crowds as large as fifty thousand people. Of all the goals we set ourselves, conquering America was by far the most glittering of prizes. However, American concert promoters weren't going to be easily convinced to book stadiums for a band with no stateside touring pedigree, regardless of our global success. So, in order to achieve this aim, our US agent played a clever game. They identified the areas where our record sales had been highest, and invited ticket applications for shows as a demonstration that we would easily fill such enormous venues. The ruse worked, and with the stadiums booked, tens of thousands of tickets were sold within hours of our shows being announced.

It wasn't just our fans that wanted to see us. Wham! was now such a big noise that we even had some big names coming to the shows.

At Hollywood Park, Fleetwood Mac star Stevie Nicks came to see us but was, inexplicably, turned away by one of our security guards, prompting a furious reaction. There was an almighty fuss and I was drafted in to try to defuse the situation. I made sure she was admitted backstage and into the show and did my best to placate an artist I regarded as a goddess. But Stevie, it has to be said, was more than slightly tired and emotional and so I'm not sure my efforts to calm her down were entirely successful.

Other celebrity encounters were a good deal more rewarding. In Miami, the Bee Gees came to our show and invited us to dinner the following day. They later showed us around the studio in which they'd recorded the soundtrack to *Saturday Night Fever*. Given our underage trip to the Watford Empire, and the countless hours we'd spent listening to their music, that day spent listening to their stories was a huge thrill for us both.

The real joy for me, though, was in simply spending time with George again. We were having a great time. The day-to-day laughing and clowning during Whamamerica! reminded me of being at school. We spent all our time on tour together, falling in and out

of scrapes, or situations where one of us might turn to the other with a look of disbelief as we wondered, *How the hell did we get into this?* One record label event saw us posing for photos with a pair of girls dressed as flamingos, for reasons that were never really explained to us.

Even travelling around the country felt surreal. For the journey to the Hollywood Park show, the promoter had arranged for us to be driven in a stretch limousine with blacked-out windows. Our trip was given an extra layer of importance by an accompanying police motorcycle escort. Dressed in aviator shades and tight uniforms straight out of the TV show *CHiPs*, four outriders flanked us, each one taking turns to accelerate away and clear the traffic ahead. George and I cringed on the floor in the back of the car, out of sight and laughing hysterically at the preposterousness of the treatment we were being given.

Living back in each other's pockets again, the in-jokes came flooding back, along with knowing looks and cheeky asides. It wasn't as if they'd ever really gone away, it was just that, apart from touring with Wham!, George and I saw less of each other socially than we used to. There was still the odd night out, but most of the time we spent together was either recording or doing promotional work. On tour, thrust back together for long uninterrupted hours, the easy intimacy and unspoken understanding of our schooldays quickly returned. But this time there was no homework to spoil it.

That the fundamentals of our friendship remained intact was possibly even more important to George than it was for me. He had never taken to life on the road with the same enthusiasm as I had. He didn't like to be away from home and the daily demands on him were so much greater than they were on me. The attention focused on George was growing, but he gradually accepted the pressure to take more interviews or make more personal appearances. It helped that George actually liked talking, and he was good at it too. During interviews together it was sometimes hard to get a word in edgeways and I was happy to let him crack on.

George seemed so enthused by the success of the American tour that it often seemed pointless to try to get my own point across, especially as he was openly discussing the possibility of a third album. 'We're just going to move on and do something different now,' he told MTV. Inspired by the quality of our touring band he sounded keen to take a more spontaneous approach. 'Well, I'd like to record a lot more of the next album live and just make it a lot more . . . I don't know . . . *less careful.*'

There was no doubt in my mind that the album he was considering had the potential to turn Wham! into one of the biggest bands of all time, but sadly it came to nothing.

Instead, we were now in the end game. And, for all the fun that he and I had enjoyed together during

Whamamerica!, he later confessed that he had found it particularly tough. We were both contemplating the future.

We had achieved everything we'd hoped for, and quickly. So quickly that we were sometimes caught off guard, especially at the speed with which America had taken to us. But as we toured the US highways, I realised that the dreams I'd once held as a kid during our first-ever gig together with The Executive had been fulfilled. There was really nowhere else to go.

I knew George was nearly at the point where he would feel comfortable going solo. His musical growing pains were almost over. *Fantastic*, *Make It Big*, the tours, Live Aid and the Apollo had provided the launch pad he needed to become George Michael, the multi-platinum, Grammy-award-winning, solo superstar.

As the character took shape, I watched him physically transform himself. The Fila shorts, cropped T-shirt and baseball cap were now a fading memory. In their place was a styling that comprised figure-hugging jeans and low-cut T-shirt, plus leather motorcycle jacket and designer stubble. The makeover really suited him. But it was all so far removed from who he really was. When we first started making music in the late 1970s, he was an awkward kid, chubby and insecure; he was confused about his sexuality and believed himself to be unattractive. That self-image took a lot of time to

shake off and it required a concerted effort to do so, but the persona he had constructed for public consumption hadn't left George with a lot of space in which to develop his true self behind the scenes. He was driven by an unstoppable desire to fulfil his potential, but that had come at a price. As a young man still trying to find himself, George's ambition to succeed had taken priority over everything else and that included his ability to openly express his sexuality.

His decision to keep that hidden only fed the uncertainty around his public persona. What the real implications of that were for George, I can't say, but I knew he was never comfortable with the added interest that came with Wham! hitting the big time. Alongside the pressure to write and perform hit songs, his personal and private life came under intense scrutiny. Everybody wanted to know who the two boys in Wham! really were. They pressed us on our friendship and any division or friction they hoped might exist between us. They asked about our family backgrounds. They wanted to know about the girls and the parties they imagined were being lavished upon us. This was fair game for a band in the public eye, but given George was adamant his sexuality should be kept under wraps, it created a wholly unwelcome extra level of stress for him to manage. It wasn't even that keeping his private life private was out of character for George. I certainly never met any boyfriend that George might have had while we were together as a band. But George feared that coming out publicly about his sexuality at the time of Whamamerica! would scupper any chances he might have of competing with artists like Madonna and Michael Jackson in the States. A terrible additional worry was the emergence of AIDS. I know I wasn't the only friend of George's who worried about him during that uncertain, frightening period. By the time George was eventually hounded into talking about his sexuality in 1998 he'd already had to mourn the loss of his partner, Anselmo Feleppa, to AIDS in 1993. It had devastated him but he'd been unable to discuss it in public. Had he spoken out earlier, who knows how differently things might have played out.

At the time, I reckoned that George opening up wouldn't have presented too much of a problem. There were so many gay people in British pop music and the record industry that his news wouldn't have raised too much of a fuss and he would have had the undying support of his closest friends. With hindsight, though, I've come to a rather different view. I'd been receiving so much unwanted attention of my own that flicking through the papers was a depressing experience. As a result I'd stopped reading tabloid gossip columns, so I was unaware of just how awful their attitudes towards gay people could be. I suspect that if George had told the truth then, every subsequent reference to him would have been prefixed by a reference to his sexuality: 'gay icon', 'gay singer' or 'gay celebrity'. While his sexuality was important to him, he wouldn't have wanted it mentioned every time someone wrote about his new record. The 1980s was a very different world to the one we live in today.

For what George was planning to do next, he needed the conditions to be perfect, both creatively and commercially. A prurient, mocking interest in his private life was the last thing he wanted. Looking back I now appreciate how naive I was about George's dilemma. For me at the time it remained a non-issue, but George's relative unease about being in the full glare of the public eye did have a bearing on how we chose to bring Wham! to a close.

After the news of our decision to bring Wham! to an end had been broken to Simon and Jazz, the only big decision left to make was what was to be done to close out Wham!'s story in the best way possible – a story that had produced so many hit records all over the world. We knew that if we were to announce a one-last-time-around-the-block tour there would be huge demand for tickets. With Simon and Jazz, I reckoned we should embark on a worldwide fare-well tour, saying goodbye to our fans around the globe and going out in a blaze of glory. I loved playing in front of a crowd. If I could, I would have toured endlessly, but George was having none of it.

'I want to do one show only,' he said, which left us

all a little confused. 'There can only be one goodbye, one final concert where Wham! bows out.'

At the time I felt he was selling the fans short. I thought we owed it to them to say farewell properly in all the countries that had embraced us with such devotion: Australia, America and Europe, among others. But George had two major concerns. Not only was he focused on his solo career, but he was also fed up with his image within Wham!. The character the band forced him to play wasn't doing him any good psychologically – it had been getting him down for quite a while and he later described Wham! as a ball and chain. It was impossible to argue with such force of feeling. I fully understood his decision and accepted it. In fact the only thing that did annoy me during that period was the cancellation of a contract we had signed with Pepsi worth over $3 million. It was a one-advert deal and there seemed no good reason not to do it, but once again George was thinking beyond Wham!. The clip was set to run for around eighteen months and so would have kept Wham! alive in the minds of the public at the very point he was trying to strike out on his own. When George pulled the plug I was angry about it as it would have helped us to recoup some of the vast expense of producing a one-off show, but in the end I reluctantly conceded that it had to go.

And so it was eventually decided that Wham! would play one show only at Wembley Stadium, a celebration of the band, which would include the premiere of *Foreign Skies*, the re-edited, reshot, remade film documentary of our Chinese adventure on the venue's big screens. Set for 28 June 1986, our farewell event was to be The Final. All that was left to do was to announce our decision to the fans. After eighteen months of speculation about George going it alone, we wanted to break the news to them on our own terms.

If only.

24. How Not To Be a Pop Star

I had realised I wanted to escape the limelight. I'd tired of the stress that accompanied life in a huge pop band and had come to resent the constant intrusions into my private life by the tabloid press. It didn't help that, for the first time in two years, I was now in a relationship. I'd met American model Donya Fiorentino in Florida.

At the time she'd been dating *Miami Vice* actor Don Johnson, but we hit it off straightaway. That we were soon together became a matter of intense interest to the media and our constant harassment at the hands of the paparazzi was troublesome. On numerous occasions in London, Donya and I were chased through the streets by snappers on motorbikes. Had George decided to make a third album with Wham! I might have felt that the attention was worthwhile, but with nothing to look forward to but The Final, and little to motivate me, I was marking time.

My situation with Donya came as a relief to George. The media fuss was just as pressurised for him, but the press were so focused on my behaviour that George flew under the radar at exactly the time he was looking ahead to a solo career. He was Wham!'s saint; I'd been painted as the sinner, but the situation suited him just fine. While the press were distracted by me, they were blind to the truth about his sexuality. The fact that George was gay had been kept well under wraps, but because he was going to gay clubs more and more, a number of people were starting to make assumptions. Within the music industry, I think Neil Tennant – the former *Smash Hits* assistant editor turned pop star with the Pet Shop Boys – might have known, and no doubt there were others. However, beyond a close inner circle nobody really had a clue, so while the reality of maintaining the façade wasn't tearing George apart, some cracks were definitely beginning to show. George still felt trapped and sometimes lashed out. On one occasion there was a scrap with his friend David Austin outside a nightclub. In another incident he pinned a photographer to a wall. A spotlight was constantly trained on him and the tight lid he held on his personal life meant his frustration could boil over.

During our early days I didn't mind the press commitments. Interviews about our music were usually fine and I was happy enough messing around in photo shoots for magazines like *Smash Hits* or *Just Seventeen*, but even I became narked when the questions turned towards my personal life. Talking about my favourite chocolate biscuit was one thing; having paparazzi photographers stalking me in restaurants and swarming around me wherever I went was quite another. You can legitimately argue that it was a two-way street. The media attention had of course been vital in propelling Wham! to stardom. I understood that, but it didn't make it any easier to cope with the relentless glare we, as household names, lived under in 1985.

Nobody advised us back then. We were in our early twenties, famous beyond our imaginations but without a mentor to guide us, or to advise us what to say or what not to say in interviews. Nobody told us where to go or where not to go. Simon and Jazz never warned us of the pitfalls of falling out of a nightclub drunk, which I did on a number of occasions. The dangers may seem obvious now, but when Wham! began I was only nineteen. Even so, the papers had all sorts of nicknames for me during the height of our fame. They called me 'Animal Andy' or 'Randy Andy', and most of the time I didn't let it bother me. I even found it amusing when girls I'd never laid eyes on gave me a ten out of ten for my performances in bed. But when I met Donya, who was a serious girlfriend, I wanted to keep our relationship off limits. Sadly not a lot of newspaper editors felt the same way and so we were hounded to the point where it made our lives a misery. I suppose what I really needed at that time was a wise head to dispense some wisdom on the pitfalls of being in the public eye. Instead I was left to figure it out for myself.

I reacted badly in situations when I should have bitten my tongue. I became snippy with journalists and then handed them the ammunition they needed to retaliate by stumbling away from parties looking visibly worse for wear. I was my own worst enemy.

With hindsight, I realise it was naive to imagine that my personal life and my public image could be separated. The two were intrinsically linked, especially once the band became a phenomenon. I should have handled the situation rather than avoiding it. But the fact was that Wham! became so big that in the end we didn't need to speak to the press to create headlines.

We only had to go to a party or a restaurant to appear in the gossip columns. One red top put us on the front page just because 'Freedom' went to number 1.

With Wham! drawing to a close, I was more than happy to escape the attention for a while. But while George was going to be carving out a new musical career for himself, the only idea I'd had for my post-Wham! life was to try my hand at motor racing.

I'd long been a fan of motorsports and as a kid I often watched the British Grand Prix whenever it was on the TV. I loved the personalities involved in Formula One during the 1970s, such as Emerson Fittipaldi, Jackie Stewart and James Hunt. There was drama and excitement in every race. Both my uncles were keen motorsports enthusiasts and used to take me and my brother to meetings at Brands Hatch. My Uncle Pete's time as a club racer only further fuelled my boyhood interest. I'd previously been invited to race in the Celebrity Car during the Renault 5 Championship where everything had gone really well until the first warm-up lap when I spun on mud on the track and into the Armco. But my interest in driving had not gone unnoticed. A motorsports promoter called Two Four Sports asked if I'd like to try out in a single-seater, having figured I might have the aptitude to take it further.

At the time, motor racing seemed far more like an exciting opportunity than a serious career. But, while it was a world away from life in Wham!, I was determined to give it my best shot – to do any less would have been a disservice to the hard graft put in by the team and their drivers. Frustratingly, there was a hitch before I'd even made it to the starting grid. After I'd shown some potential in test drives, I committed to a full season of racing, but, after I'd signed the deal, it was pointed out that my insurance contract as a performer – a performer who was set to play Wembley Stadium the next summer – prevented me from taking part in dangerous sports like skydiving, skiing or, of course, any form of motor racing. And so, for the three months before The Final, I couldn't race. It was an ignominious start and proved to be a setback from which my season never recovered.

I remained committed to my new endeavour, however,

travelling down to the Nogaro circuit in south-west France for pre-season testing in early 1986. Then, out of the blue, the shit hit the fan. On a cold, damp February morning, I sat in my race car for the first time, nervously eyeing the track ahead of me. A frosting of ice had coated the tarmac, increasing the chances of a spin or an accident. As I prepared to head down the pit lane onto the track, a circuit official leant over the cockpit.

'Er, Mr Ridgeley, we have a phone call for you in race control. It's your lawyer in London.'

It beggared belief. As if the prospect of flying around an icy race circuit at insane speeds wasn't stressful enough, I was unexpectedly being hassled from England. Unbuckling my seatbelt, I went upstairs where I was told the news: George had sacked Simon and Jazz. After learning that Wham! was splitting, our managers had decided to sell off their management company for five million quid to a company that was partially owned by South African businessman Sol Kerzner, the man behind the controversial Sun City resort. The news caused George to explode. The 'WHAM! SOLD TO SUN CITY' headline didn't help matters. Simon later said that he was unaware of the links with apartheid South Africa and, in fairness to him, it was a rare and uncharacteristic mistake. Sadly for him, though, it was a terminal one. As George and I approached one of the most important moments in our musical career so far, we were suddenly rudderless.

'What do you want to do?' asked the lawyer nervously. 'They're waiting for your answer . . .'

I was dumbfounded. I was about to drive a Formula Three car for the first time in the worst conditions possible and a bomb had been dropped in my lap. I experienced a terrible sinking feeling. '*What do I want to do?* Well, it would be nice to disappear off the face of the planet! I need some time to think.'

In the end I left the problem to poor George, but that too had unintended consequences. The fallout was a nightmare. During a press statement announcing our split from Simon and Jazz, it was also assumed that George and I were breaking up. And while, for once, the assumptions were correct, it put paid to our plans to announce bringing the band to an end in a manner of our choosing. Headlines announcing our split dominated the news. George was then forced into admitting the truth by revealing we were playing a farewell show later in the year, while at the same time having to explain my absence.

'Unfortunately Andrew was racing in Monaco,' he told chat-show host Michael Aspel. 'So what happened was that the statement came across as something about me leaving Andrew behind as opposed to [leaving] the management behind, which was really not the case. And Andrew and I are meeting up next week in Los Angeles to record the last Wham! single and the concert hopefully will go ahead . . . There's absolutely no rift whatsoever between the two of us. It's just something that the press have been waiting for for so long . . . I think it should be the most amicable split in pop history if we do it properly.'

When the tickets eventually went on sale, a million fans jammed the box office phone lines. Wham! could have sold out Wembley a dozen times over and still not satisfied demand.

The Final was the hottest ticket of the year.

Our last single, 'The Edge Of Heaven', was released on 18 June 1986. An overtly sexual track, it features lines such as:

> I'm like a maniac, at the end of the day
> I'm like a doggie barking at your door.

And like a lot of George's later material with Wham!, it had a timeless appeal, bursting with vitality. As we'd played it throughout the Whamamerica! tour the previous year, 'The Edge Of Heaven' became my favourite song to perform live.

In terms of image, the song's video helped establish the classic George Michael look, which he would carry on into his debut solo album the following year: leather biker jacket, designer stubble. His evolution towards solo superstar was gathering pace, while for Wham! it was the end of the road.

And I still couldn't help feeling that, in a way, we'd betrayed our fans. The fact we were only doing one farewell show had, as I've said, annoyed me. Touring the world one last time, while still only satisfying a fraction of the international demand, would have been an amazing opportunity. Sadly, George was spent. Emotionally exhausted by Wham!, the thought of travelling across America again, playing the likes of 'Bad Boys' or 'Young Guns', was too much. And in truth, although I wanted to play more shows, perhaps I'd had enough too. I really couldn't face the endless press and TV and the intense scrutiny of my private life that would have come with another tour. For the time being, escape became my new focus.

After Wham! played two warm-up shows at Brixton Academy, the big day was finally upon us. And, typically enough, I was late. I'd been staying at a friend's house in Rickmansworth for a few weeks while Wham! ran through rehearsals and pre-production for The Final. Planning on travelling to the show with a few friends, I decided to hire a car for the trip to Wembley, but our timing was off. We were behind schedule, but after racing through London's suburbs, I was relieved to finally see the famous twin towers in the distance. That was when the flashing lights of a police car suddenly appeared in my rear-view mirror, ordering me to pull over. I'd been speeding. The ticking-off was excruciating. We were a stone's throw from Wembley Park

Station as tens of thousands of Wham! fans spilled out towards Wembley Way. I parked up behind a coachload of youngsters in Wham! T-shirts, unaware of what was happening just outside their window.

'Do you know how fast you were travelling, sir?' asked the policeman, pulling out his notepad.

I glanced up. A girl on the back seat of the coach had realised what was going on. She was staring at me open-mouthed, as if she was trying to scream, but couldn't.

'Er, officer . . . I don't mean to be rude, but I'm actually playing a concert here tonight and I'm a bit late.' I pointed up at the bus ahead, sensing that pandemonium was about to break out.

The penny dropped. 'Are you . . . ?' said the policeman. 'Oh, I see, yes, well, Mr Ridgeley, we'll write this one off as happening under extenuating circumstances.'

He scribbled a note in his pad. 'I'm still giving you a ticket, mind.'

I happily took the hit and got moving. Points and a fine paled into insignificance next to the prospect of getting mobbed outside the stadium.

The mood behind the scenes at The Final was uncannily familiar. While Pepsi and Shirlie got ready in their dressing room, the smell of singeing hair wafted out from where George and I prepared ourselves. Would this be the last time I sat through him scorching his barnet with a pair of straighteners? I wasn't nervous – I rarely experienced nerves before a show – but any sense that we were coming to the end of an era was dissipated by the happy, relaxed atmosphere backstage. As the re-edited version of *Foreign Skies* premiered in front of a record-breaking Wembley crowd, George and I were interviewed backstage.

What about the fans? It's a thank you concert, isn't it?

'A big thank you,' I said. 'Especially to the people who didn't manage to get tickets. We would have loved to have seen everyone off . . .'

So, no regrets about splitting up?

'None whatsoever,' said George.

As the camera rolled, I pretended to throttle him.

According to George, at the show's close he experienced a wash of sadness as we walked back to our dressing room, leaving behind an arena full of screaming fans. A chapter had been shut on our lives, and the moment was tinged with pain. There was the sense that our relationship would never be the same again, no matter what happened. I could understand his mood in some ways. Life was going to be very different for us both as we went our separate ways, having spent the previous ten years together as schoolboys and then bandmates. But I also believed the essence of our relationship wouldn't shift in any way. We weren't breaking up as friends, and in the hours after The Final, George and I were going to a party together as best mates.

In the programme notes for the show I'd written: 'We all wake up in the middle of our dreams.' Part of me felt as if I'd been in some weird *Twilight Zone* for months, sleepwalking towards this moment. But this was it.

Wham! was done.

As summer turned to autumn, we didn't see as much of each other as we had, but when we did, things were much as they ever were. The same in-jokes made us laugh; we bickered and sparred with each other just as we always had; and still neither of us was prepared to concede the last word. It was clear to us both that our friendship would endure, and yet sometimes I worried for my friend.

I visited George in America a few months after The Final and noticed his mood was quite heavy. I think he was in the middle of writing *Faith* at that point. We went out a few times and had some fairly late nights, and in the middle of my stay he played the album track 'Kissing A Fool'. I was absolutely knocked out by it. I loved it from the very first listen and thought it indicated the bright, exciting future ahead for George. But despite the fact that he was now free to fulfil his ambition to be the solo artist he so wanted to be, he seemed troubled; self-doubt had returned. While his confidence had grown as Wham! had been wound down, George was now struggling with what being George Michael truly meant. What had he become? He was bothered about whether or not it was something he could live with.

George still didn't feel that he could publicly acknowledge his sexuality, but following the path he'd chosen meant he would only become more and more famous. Facing everything that further success would entail seemed daunting – it was set to be so much more stressful than anything he had experienced in Wham!. I was honest with him. I told him what he almost certainly already knew: that if he were to stand any chance of finding happiness he would have to fulfil his talent;

and that writing music was really the only thing that gave him any satisfaction and contentment. He really didn't have a choice. I knew there was only one thing for George to do next, and that was to claim his place as the greatest singer-songwriter of his generation.

25. You Have Been Loved

My life after Wham! took one or two unexpected turns. My turn as a Formula Three driver was fairly short-lived. During my first season in 1986 I crashed more times than I finished races and my poor crew had to rebuild the car through the night on more than one occasion.

Any thoughts of an acting career also amounted to nothing when an acting coach tried to get me to cry by proposing that I imagine my mother had died. After that, and despite one or two Hollywood offers, it wasn't something that I could see myself enjoying. Given how much I had hated the process of making videos, I probably should have anticipated that!

But in 1988 I started writing songs again and, after playing a couple of demos to Wham!'s old label, Epic, they suggested I make an album. I wanted to test the water with a single, but the economics of the industry had changed, which meant a release only made sense if it was backed up by an LP.

So the next year I returned to the studio to record my own solo album, *Son Of Albert*. It felt good. The recording process, spread out over a year or so, was rewarding and great fun too, taking place at various studios across London and LA. One track, 'Shake', was written with David Austin, my former bandmate from The Executive. On another, 'Red Dress', George suggested contributing backing vocals after hearing a rough mix and liking what he heard. When he popped by to lend a hand, I was struggling with a vocal for the bridge. He jumped straight in and we nailed the part in short order, recording my lead before adding George's backing vocals. He came down to the studio and took the reins, running the mixing desk like he owned the place. It was just like old times.

But by that time George had become a massive solo success in his own right. His first album, *Faith*, was released in 1987, and established him as the performer he'd always wanted to be. Dressed in his leathers, figure-hugging denim and aviator shades, George now looked the part, but, as ever, it was the quality of the songs that underpinned it all. Songs like 'I Want Your Sex', 'Faith', 'Father Figure' and 'Kissing A Fool', the song he'd played me as he'd been working on it, attracted an audience so very different to the teenage girls who had once thrown their underwear at us on the Club Fantastic tour.

George now had total command over his own recording process but, despite applying a little bit of that stardust to 'Red Dress', it didn't help *Son Of Albert* in the long run. The album barely dented the UK charts and only in Australia did the lead single, 'Shake', make the Top 20. It was a very disappointing end to things and, shortly afterwards, I decided I'd had enough of the music business for good.

There was to be one notable exception, however.

At the beginning of 1991, George embarked on his second solo tour. Playing dates in North and South America, Japan, Canada and the UK, he labelled it the Cover to Cover tour. Along with some choice tracks from *Faith* and from Wham!, George crammed the show with his own interpretations of some of the songs he loved most, from the Eagles to Stevie Wonder, from 'Papa Was A Rolling Stone' to 'Lady Marmalade'.

I was lucky enough to go along to the rehearsals for the show and was blown away by his version of the Doobie Brothers' 'What A Fool Believes'. One of George's talents as a singer was his ability to mimic the very best. Even as a fourteen- or fifteen-year-old, he could step up to the tape recorder in his bedroom and match the likes of Freddie and Elton. Now, as I stood there, stunned, he ran through a song that everybody knew was one of the toughest for anyone to capture. Michael McDonald had put in a virtuoso performance on the original recording, but here was George singing it every bit as well, if not better. I would soon have an opportunity to see its effect on a live audience.

After opening his tour with a couple of dates at the Birmingham NEC, George flew out to Brazil to headline the massive Rock in Rio festival. And he'd invited me to join him onstage in front of an audience of nearly two hundred thousand people in the Maracaña Stadium. It made Wembley Stadium look like a village fete. I was struggling with a chest infection at the time, which took some of the shine off what was otherwise a joyful revival of old times. It was so great to strap on a guitar and be up there performing alongside George again as he approached the peak of his powers. We played 'I'm Your Man', and then followed it with 'Freedom '90' from George's second solo album, *Listen Without Prejudice Vol. 1*. To play together on one last occasion in front of our biggest-ever audience felt fitting. And to share in the same performance of a song which spoke directly about how George had moved on from our time in Wham! represented the perfect coda to our band's story.

George's Cover to Cover tour went on to provide a wonderful showcase for his boundless talent as a singer of other people's songs. And it would be a cover version, performed in front of a global audience, which would provide one of the most memorable moments of George's career as a solo artist.

Freddie Mercury passed away from AIDS in November 1991. The following April, the remaining members of Queen – guitarist Brian May, drummer Roger Taylor and bassist John Deacon – pulled together a concert with all proceeds going to AIDS research. In place of Freddie, his bandmates played with a line-up of A-list singers including David Bowie, Elton John, Annie Lennox, Axl Rose and Robert Plant. And George, who had been invited to sing 'Somebody To Love'. It was a song he'd adored and Freddie would have known just how much it had meant to both of us growing up. It encapsulated everything George loved about the band. Freddie's vocal was incredible and the song is one of Queen's best, but George also loved the references to classical music that were buried under the guitars. George and I had spoken about it many times. And while I'd missed my opportunity to tell Freddie that at Live Aid, I did at least get the chance to tell Brian May when I sat next to him at one of Elton's parties. Over dinner, he very kindly let me prattle on excitedly about how great they had been at Ally Pally in 1979 and how important his band had been to me as a kid.

Stepping into Freddie's shoes at Wembley would have been incredibly tough for George, but there were only a handful of artists that could even have contemplated it. To perform a song by one of his idols at Wembley Stadium, backed by Queen themselves, would have been thrilling. That Freddie had been taken too soon by a cruel disease weighted it with emotion.

At the time of the show, I was driving back from Donington racetrack where I'd been watching a round of the Superbike World Championship. The tribute show was broadcast live on the radio and I was heading south down the M1 when George was announced onstage. The roars of the crowd echoing around Wembley filled the car. I turned up the volume and listened as he delivered a magnificent performance that gave me goosebumps. It was powerful, moving and incredibly emotional, and George's vocals amazed me. Just as 'Don't Let The Sun Go Down On Me' at Live Aid had allowed him to demonstrate to everybody just what he was capable of as a singer, so 'Somebody To Love' was a showcase which, strangely enough, I didn't think his own songs provided to quite the same extent. Hearing my best friend sing a track that we'd been in awe of together was one of the most moving musical moments of my life.

Just for a second there was a pang of yearning, too. I wanted to be there, performing. It wasn't a feeling of envy or regret, but just the realisation that I missed being onstage, playing in front of a huge crowd hanging on my every move. It momentarily reignited an old desire. As I'd grown older, and my time in Wham! receded, those sensations had become more fleeting, but as I drove home along the motorway that day they once again seemed very real.

I never acted on them. That last appearance onstage with George in Rio would remain *my* Final.

At around four o'clock in the afternoon on Christmas Day 2016, my mobile phone rang. I was in London spending

Christmas with friends and I'd just texted George. He'd
sent me his annual Christmas hamper, which had been
a tradition for him for years, a box stuffed with all sorts
of treats, and I wanted to thank him for it. 'Yog, thanks,
as always, for the hamper!' I wrote. 'I hope you're having
fun over the festive season. Hope to catch up in the new
year, let me know where you'll be/when you'll be. A xx.'
Not five minutes later, my phone rang. It was George's
sister, Melanie. I honestly thought that she was calling to

wish me a happy Christmas, or that maybe she was with George and the family, and they were ringing to arrange a get-together. There was certainly nothing to hint at the awful news which followed.

'Andrew, I hate to tell you this,' said Melanie. 'But George has died.'

The news hit me like a punch to the gut. It was as if my world had been pulled out from underneath me. I felt overwhelmed and couldn't quite comprehend what was being said. The details and hows and wheres rushed by. My best friend had died on Christmas Day and now his sister was having to tell me on the phone. I couldn't imagine how hard that must have been for her, to have to call so many people at home and tell the same dreadful news over and over. But Melanie managed to hold herself together and delivered the details with great dignity.

I put down the phone and, doubled over in grief, began to sob.

And on Christmas Day, too. George had loved Christmas, and 'Last Christmas' had become an annual reminder that the festive season was approaching. Over thirty years on from its original release, its melodies were inescapable. Every year it crept back onto radio playlists because George had achieved his aim of writing a timeless classic. Like Paul McCartney's 'Wonderful Christmastime' or Slade's 'Merry Xmas Everybody', the song was synonymous with everything people embraced at that time of year: family, sharing, celebration and love.

334

Now it was set to be a reminder of George's passing.

I called friends to tell them the news. I was shaken; the reality felt catastrophic and it was hard to get a handle on what had happened. For the next couple of days I felt lost and stayed in London because the press had descended upon my home in Cornwall. But I wasn't in a position to talk about George at that time. I felt crushed by sadness. There was talk of a newspaper charity campaign to get 'Last Christmas' to number 1, but neither George's family nor I would give it our blessing in view of the appalling way some of them had treated him, not least once details surrounding his death began to leak out. People took to social media to give voice to their opinions and feelings. That the circumstances of his death seemed unclear only compounded the distress. Without any real closure, the grieving seemed terribly raw. A heart condition was eventually recorded as the cause of death, but there were still a number of questions. He seemed to be in good health at the time and there are conflicting reports surrounding the night that preceded his passing. It now seems as if we may never know what really happened. We don't live our lives being monitored, so when someone dies alone, perhaps there are always answers that remain out of reach. It still feels uncomfortable, though. God knows what it must be like for George's family.

It became a matter of the utmost importance to me that I paid tribute to George at the Brit Awards in

February 2017. I felt privileged to have been asked, and honoured. The speech was something I had to do. To my mind, I needed to speak on behalf of George's fans and for the public. I knew at that point there wasn't going to be a public memorial service for the fans, but the people who had loved George and his music needed some sense of closure. I felt for those fans – those people with nothing tangible to hold on to in the fallout of his death. I felt a responsibility for that and so my speech at the Brits mattered greatly.

Both Pepsi and Shirlie felt the same way and they joined me at the O2 to pay their respects to George in front of a packed audience. Shirlie was incredibly upset and found the event very difficult, but it was the right thing for the three of us to do and essential that we give public voice to the love and grief which was felt by all. At times during Wham! the camaraderie between the four of us had been intense. We had felt like a family. Seeing the three of us together reminded everyone that they had been part of that family too. Wham! had always been as much about them as it was about us. And we were united in wanting to acknowledge the impact that George had had on us all.

'On Christmas Day 2016, the greatest singer-songwriter of his generation, an icon of his era, and my beloved friend, George Michael, was lost,' I said. 'A supernova in a firmament of shining stars had been extinguished and it felt like the sky had fallen in . . .

'George's contribution to the great archive of contemporary music rests alongside the immortals . . . George has left for us in his songs, in the transcendental beauty of his voice, and in the poetic expression of his soul, the very best of himself.

'I loved him and in turn, we, you, have been loved.'

A little over a month later, we attended the funeral in North London. It was an elegant, understated and tasteful occasion at which George's younger sister Melanie spoke very movingly on behalf of her brother, but her eulogy was not quite what I'd expected. She spoke of how much his closest friends had meant to him throughout his life. It was a particularly poignant moment for me in a ceremony that was so different to those I'd attended before. And as I watched George being lowered into the ground the emotion became overwhelming. All of us dropped white roses on his coffin as we passed.

Despite the pain of his death, George is still very much alive in my memory today. A few years on from that tragic Christmas, I'll sometimes catch myself thinking of our friendship and those years together as young kids in Wham!. There are constant reminders everywhere. I might hear a single on the radio, especially when 'Last Christmas' makes its regular return.

Every now and then a headline appears that takes me back to a moment we shared. In those instances, it's always our friendship that I miss, rather than any musical or cultural event. And more often than not I'll remember the laughs we enjoyed together when we were on our own in a bar chatting over a beer, or backstage, travelling or just messing around in each other's company.

When it was just the two of us.

George was great company when he was able to be himself – off duty, at home or on holiday, when he felt comfortable and relaxed. I was lucky to be around him a lot during those times. I was lucky too to share with him the unspoken understanding that exists between best friends. Undoubtedly, George was my best friend. And I've not had as strong a bond with any other chum since then. After first meeting George – when he was Yog – at school we spent the next ten years living in each other's pockets, mucking around in and out of class and then making music together. I've discovered that type of intensity is harder to rediscover as you get older.

I don't think our friendship was any different to millions of others between kids our age; it's just that through Wham! ours was carried on into adulthood and played out for everyone to see. Our friendship struck a chord with people because they saw something in us that they recognised, or aspired to in their own lives. And although as we grew older we were living in different worlds, forty years later the depth of feeling we'd had for each other was undimmed. Back then, in September 1975, he had been Georgios Panayiotou – *the*

New Boy – unsure of himself, with an unruly haircut and unfashionable specs. By the time he'd transformed into George Michael several years later, he and Wham! had reshaped my life forever. Now I'm left with the music we made together, the videos on YouTube and a mountain of scrapbooks brimming with magazine cuttings and newspaper exclusives saved by my mum. And the memories of a golden friendship.

For a brief while, Wham! had been one of the biggest bands on the planet and a pop sensation. Most of all, George and I had been the best of friends. Two boys that made hit singles together, saw the world and had the time of their lives – and in whose friendship the world saw love, life and laughter.

Acknowledgements

I'd like to express special thanks to the following people for their part in the realisation of this
endeavour:

Jonny Fowler at Jon Fowler Media for making a con-
vincing case for doing a memoir and for his steadfast
loyalty. Tim Bates at PFD for his unflappable sang-
froid. Matt Allen for admirable skills on the end of a
hospital pass.

All at Michael Joseph, Penguin Random House,
but in particular: Louise Moore for her belief in this
memoir; Rowland White and Beatrix McIntyre for
working an editorial miracle; Emma Plater for her
cheeriness and judgement in piecing the whole thing
together; Roy McMillan for his expert guidance and
a light touch; Liz Smith, Clare Parker, Gaby Young,
Vicky Photiou and the marketing and promo teams for
their sterling work; Jill Schwartzman for her support
and enthusiasm; Emma D'Cruz and Matthew Blackett
for being reasonable and accommodating; James Keyte
and Catherine Le Lievre for their help and assistance
along the way.

Seb Davey and Stephen Tregear at Russells for, in

the first instance, his diligence and infinite patience, and in the second, giving no quarter.

The team at Peters Fraser & Dunlop, particularly Alexandra Cliff and the foreign rights team and Laura McNeill.

Picture Credits

The author and publisher would like to thank all copyright holders for permission to reproduce their work. Every effort has been made to trace copyright holders and to obtain their permission for the use of copyright material. The publisher apologizes for any errors or omissions and would be grateful to be notified of any corrections that should be incorporated in future editions of this book.

Introduction

p. 3 © PA Images; p. 4 supplied by author, copyright unknown; p. 5 supplied by author, copyright unknown; p. 9 © Michael Putland/Getty Images; p. 10 © Topfoto; p. 14 © Michael Putland/Getty Images; p. 18 © Mirrorpix

Chapter 1

p. 25 © Pete Still/Redferns/Getty Images

Chapter 2

p. 35 top © Martyn Goddard, bottom © Albert Ridgeley

345

Chapter 3

p. 44 top © Albert Ridgeley, bottom: author's own; p. 45 top and bottom © Albert Ridgeley; p. 49 top © Albert Ridgeley, bottom: author's own

Chapter 4

p. 59 © Albert Ridgeley; p. 61 author's own; p. 64 via Flickr

Chapter 5

p. 72 Author's own; p. 83 © Mirrorpix

Chapter 6

p. 89 top © Simon Hanhart, bottom © Michael Burdett; p. 95 © Albert Ridgeley

Chapter 7

p. 99 top © Jeffrey Blackler/Alamy Stock Photo, bottom left and right © Albert Ridgeley

Chapter 8

p. 113 supplied by author, copyright unknown; p. 115 ©
Mirrorpix; p. 116 © Albert Ridgeley

Chapter 9

p. 125 © Topfoto; p. 127 © Topfoto; p. 129 top © Topfoto,
bottom © FG/Bauer-Griffin/Getty Images

Chapter 10

p. 132 © Albert Ridgeley; p. 133 author's own; p. 138 © Topfoto; p. 143 © Albert Ridgeley

Chapter 11

p. 149 © Ian Dickson/Redferns/Getty Images; p. 152 top
© Michael Putland, bottom © Gabor Scott/Redferns/
Getty Images; p. 154 © Alamy; p. 161 © Mirrorpix

Chapter 12

p. 165 © David Clarke/BBC Photo Sales; p. 166 © David
Clarke/BBC Photo Sales; p. 171 © Alamy; p. 172 ©
Mirrorpix

Chapter 13

p. 179 © Topfoto; p. 180 © Martyn Goddard; p. 183 © Albert Ridgeley

Chapter 14

p. 191 top © Topfoto, bottom © Topfoto

Chapter 15

p. 202 © Pete Cronin/Redferns/Getty Images; p. 206 © Globe Photos/Zuma Press/PA Images

Chapter 16

p. 209 top © Michael Putland/Getty Images, bottom © PA/PA Archive/PA Images; p. 213 top © Michael Putland; p. 215 © John Swannell; p. 218 © Michael Putland/Getty Images; p. 220 author's own; p. 221 © Albert Ridgeley

Chapter 17

p. 227 © Michael Putland; p. 234 © The Sun/News Licensing; p. 236 © Mirrorpix; p. 239 © Rogers/Stringer/Hulton Archive/Getty Images

Chapter 18

p. 243 © Mirrorpix; p. 245 © Albert Ridgeley

Chapter 19

p. 257 © Daily Express/Express Syndication

Chapter 20

p. 264 © John Swannell; p. 266 © Michael Putland/Getty Images

Chapter 21

p. 268 © Mirrorpix/Getty Images; p. 269 © Kent Gavin/Mirrorpix; p. 270 top and bottom © Albert Ridgeley; p. 272 © Neal Preston; p. 278 © Daily Express/Express Syndication

Chapter 22

p. 282 © Chris Craymer; p. 285 top © Georges De Keerle/Getty Images; p. 287 top © Topfoto, bottom © Topfoto; p. 288 © Michael Putland/Getty Images; p. 294 © Neil Leifer/Sports Illustrated via Getty Images; p. 295 © FG/Bauer-Griffin/Getty Images

Chapter 23

p. 301 © Chris Craymer; p. 305 © Chris Craymer; p. 309 © Albert Ridgeley

Chapter 24

p. 311 © Dave Hogan/Getty Images; p. 315 supplied by author, copyright unknown; p. 320 © Topfoto; p. 324 © Mirrorpix; p. 326 © Mirrorpix

Chapter 25

p. 333 © Mirrorpix; p. 336 © Karwai Tang/WireImage/ Getty Images; p. 340 © Mirrorpix; p. 341 © Mirrorpix

First colour section

p. 1 top © Albert Ridgeley; middle © Jennifer Ridgeley; bottom: author's own

p. 2 top left: author's own; top right © Albert Ridgeley; bottom © Albert Ridgeley

p. 3 top left © Albert Ridgeley; top right © Albert Ridgeley; bottom: author's own

p. 4 top © Albert Ridgeley; bottom left © Albert Ridgeley; bottom right © Jennifer Ridgeley

p. 5 top supplied by author, copyright unknown; bottom © Albert Ridgeley

p. 6 both © Albert Ridgeley

p. 7 top supplied by author, copyright unknown; bottom © Albert Ridgeley

p. 8 both author's own

Second colour section

p. 1 top supplied by author, copyright unknown; bottom left supplied by author, copyright unknown; bottom right © Mirrorpix

p. 2 top author's own; middle supplied by author, copyright unknown; bottom © Martyn Goddard

p. 3 top © Albert Ridgeley; bottom © Martyn Goddard

p. 4 top © Martyn Goddard; bottom left © Martyn Goddard; bottom right supplied by author, copyright unknown

p. 5 top © Photoshot/TopFoto; middle © Phil Dent/Redferns/Getty Images; bottom right © Chris Craymer

p. 6 top supplied by author, copyright unknown; middle supplied by author, copyright unknown; bottom © Albert Ridgeley

p. 7 all four images © Chris Craymer

p. 8 top © John Swannell; middle © John Swannell; bottom © Michael Putland/Getty Images

Third colour section

p. 2 top supplied by author, copyright unknown; bottom © Mike Maloney/Shutterstock

p. 3 top left © Topfoto; top right © Mirrorpix/Getty Images; bottom © Topfoto

p. 4 top © Getty Images; middle © Mirrorpix; bottom © Topfoto

p. 5 top left © Mirrorpix; top right © Topfoto; bottom © Mirrorpix/Getty Images

p. 6 top © Alan Olley/Mirrorpix/Getty Images; bottom © Topfoto

p. 7 top © Mick Hutson/Redferns/Getty Images; bottom © Karwai Tang/WireImage/Getty Images

p. 8 © Roger Bamber/Shutterstock